Town Union Governance
A Community Service in Eastern Nigeria

Felix I. Nweke

i

Adonis & Abbey Publishers Ltd
St James House
13 Kensington Square,
London, W8 5HD
United Kingdom

Website: http://www.adonis-abbey.com
E-mail Address: editor@adonis-abbey.com

Nigeria:
Suites C4 & C5 J-Plus Plaza
Asokoro, Abuja, Nigeria
Tel: +234 (0) 7058078841/08052035034

British Library Cataloguing-in-Publication Data
A catalogue record for this book is available from the British Library

ISBN: 978-1-909112-65-0

Town Union Governance
A Community Service in Eastern Nigeria

Felix I. Nweke

Table of contents

All of you who helped me in my growing up years
I see you on my memory lane
You have not changed.

Felix I. Nweke

Dedications

To

J. O. Ibik, G. C. Odumodu, I. M Anah, Okonkwo Agbaloko Okwuogu and others who supported the people of Ukpo Dunukofia community with integrity and patience throughout many years of the community's struggle for justice.

To

John Achebe, John Mezue, Emmanuel Onuegbu, Anthony Onyeka, Christian Chife, Augustine Esedo and others who in their postings as pioneer teachers worked with commitment and laid the foundation for corps of educated men and women of Ukpo Dunukofia origin.

Endorsements

Professor Felix Nweke narrated the account of a self-help community service in Eastern Nigeria with the experience of an insider and proficiency of a writer. A major concern in the book is that government involvement in town union affairs will compromise the foundational element of the organization, namely the self-help element.

Mrs Ngozi Ajuonu,
Founder and Chief Executive, Rural Women Foundation.

This book calls attention to an ongoing phenomenon in Africa, which is the process of transition from rural to urban societies by various communities following the rapid economic growth in most of the countries in the continent. The book points at the impacts of poverty, increasing inequality and wide income gaps which are a consequence of the transition from rural to urban societies.

Dr. Werner Kiene,
Former Ford Foundation Program Officer in Nigeria.

Professor Nweke wrote this book with the characteristic candidness and boldness, the virtues for which he is known in the Ukpo Dunukofia community. As President General of the Town Union he helped to resolve the conflicts between our community and two neighboring communities without violence.

Dr. Robert C. Eze,
Traditional Leader,
Ukpo Dunukofia.

Foreword

The town union democratic governance is indigenous among Igbo people. Its formalization and recognition as part of the fourth tier of government in the states of the South-East geopolitical zone of Nigeria is a recent development and is still evolving. As the author explains in the case of his community it is correct to state that in the various communities in Eastern Nigeria the relationship between the elected democratic town union government and the monarchy is still being worked out. There are opportunities in the democratic town union system in terms of improved governance in Eastern Nigeria particularly because of the strong rural base which makes the town union a grassroots system of governance. The opportunities make the experiment in town union governance worthwhile in Nigeria.

Town Union Governance: A Community Service in Eastern Nigeria is a definitive book. The book is the first of its kind in town union governance in the South-East geopolitical zone of Nigeria. The book shows that town union governments can be of assistance to the state government in maintaining peace and order in various communities; in settling tensions and conflicts between communities without violence; in creating awareness among community members for the need to respect the environment; and in bringing to the attention of the state government the needs of the communities in the various sectors of community life such as health, education, and so on. The poverty impact of the process of transition from rural to urban societies following rapid economic and population growths as highlighted in the book should be of concern to Nigerian political leaders and policy makers and to international donor organizations and Non-Governmental Organizations.

The book defines the virtues of leadership that are needed for a town union government in a rural setting to perform and achieve its functional goals. The chapters on sustainability concerns and lessons learned document what are to be expected in terms of challenges by would-be town union government officials. The concluding argument of the chapter on lessons learned is thought provoking. The future of the system as a self-help organization depends on finding a solution to revenue generation that will preserve the basic element of self-help. This conclusion is backed by the author's experience as the President General of the town union of his community for three years from 2006 to 2008.

Town union government officials should read this book. More documentations of the type of the book are necessary to enable the town union governments to learn from each other's experiences and lead to continued evolution of the system of governance.

Hon. Paul C. Okeke
Member Anambra State House of Assembly from 1999 to 2007

Acknowledgements

As a documentary on the interventions of town union government of Ukpo Dunukofia community from 2006 to 2008 this book tells the story of the people of that community. For that reason all members of the community including members who opposed various initiatives of the town union government contributed to the formation of the book. Voices of opposition kept the government alert to its responsibilities as well as focused on most important problems of the community. The programs of the government were ambitious, expensive, and intensive requiring active participation of members of the community. Freewill contributions of money, time, ideas and services made by some of the community members made it possible for the town union government to execute its programs successfully.

Without remunerations, members of the central executive of the town union government carried out their assigned functions with considerable commitment at the expense of their personal businesses. They did not complain about long hours of scheduled monthly and numerous emergency meetings. They spoke their minds freely often with enthusiasm on matters tabled before them. The town union government consulted extensively with the cabinet of the traditional leader on important matters of the community. Members of the cabinet made constructive contributions in terms of ideas that enriched the work of the town union government.

Kingsley Osondu Ezeaku, Eugene Otunabo, Samuel Ugoezue, Samuel Ifeacho, Godson Ofora, Eric Omejilichi and Elias Afoemeka Okafor assisted with collection of information. Robert C. Eze and Chukwudi Chikelue read the manuscript and made valuable suggestions. When the author was writing this book Paul C. Okeke provided him free board and lodging in his Lone Palm hotel in Asaba for extended periods of time. Charles Ezeunala, Sunny Nwachukwu and Chinyere Okunna provided support to the author.

All these people and more deserve acknowledgement.

Introduction

The rapid economic growth that is taking place across African countries at present means that all over the continent there are communities that are in the process of transition from rural to urban societies. Physical appearances of such communities convey a false sense of affluence because of the presence of a relatively few modern homes and small businesses that are springing up in such communities. Beneath those appearances, widespread destitution is compounded by relativity of poverty which becomes acute where the rich and the poor share the same neighborhoods[1]. In transitional societies needs for improvements in basic necessities of the people are monumental and the burden weighs heavily on the poor.

The well-to-do households secure their homes with hired security guards; they have electricity generating plants and water boreholes in their homes; they send their children to elite schools outside the area; and they have access to hospitals in the urban centers. In the past when everybody lived in thatched houses, went about their businesses on foot, drew water from the same spring, etc. poverty was not an issue since everyone was poor. The influence of relativity of poverty combines with urbanization problems such as high cost of living to add to the strong case that can be made for poverty alleviation programs in transitional societies. People aspire for what they are aware of and some welcome opportunities to realize their aspirations through criminal means. For that reason transitional communities are fertile grounds for recruitment of criminals.

Prevalent poverty in transitional communities which are widespread in Africa faults agricultural R&D (research and development) initiatives that focus poverty alleviation programs on smallholder farmers while denying pervasive poverty among urban consumers. That denial prompts the question: What is the aim of poverty focus in agricultural R&D initiatives? Is it to sustain smallholder farmers in poverty or to lift them out of poverty? In Africa, agricultural R&D initiatives emphasize the development and dissemination of technologies that increase crop and

---

[1] Relativity of poverty derives from the fact that poverty is relative. Where everybody is poor the impact is not felt. But where the poor live side by side with the rich the impact of poverty becomes intense.

livestock yields so that the smallholders will have enough to eat while they remain in poverty. Mechanical labor-saving technologies that can lift smallholders out of poverty by reducing production costs and by driving down consumer prices are ignored by international donor organizations, national political leaders and policy makers as non-smallholder technologies or on the wrong assumption of surplus labor in African agriculture.

This book is a documentation of the author's direct experience as the leader of a rural community based self-help development organization in Eastern Nigeria from 2006 to 2008. The aim of the book is to draw the attention of African national governments, international donor organizations, and NGOs (Non-Governmental Organizations) to the desperate problems of the poor in societies that are in transition from rural to urban communities which are increasing in numbers in Africa. The book is the first of its kind on the subject it addresses and in the geographical area it represents, namely Eastern Nigeria.

Nigeria has 36 states that are grouped into six geopolitical zones: Middle-Belt, North-East, North-West, South-East, South-South, and South-West. The grouping is based mostly on ethnicity. The South-East geopolitical zone is made up of five of the 36 states that are homogeneous in terms of having only Igbo people as their indigenous population and in terms of having a different style of fourth tier of government than states in the other geopolitical zones. In practice Nigeria as a whole has four tiers of government, namely federal, state, local, and community. The third tier is referred to as Local Government Area and each is made up of a number of communities. The fourth tier is a diarchy in the five South-East states and a monarchy in the rest of the states in the country[2]. Each community in the South-East geopolitical zone like communities in other geopolitical zones has a traditional leadership which is monarchy. But unlike communities in the other zones, communities in the South-East have, in addition democratically elected town union governments side by side with and parallel to the monarchy[3].

Monarchy form of government is a relatively new development among Igbo people. Customarily Igbo communities were governed

---

[2] Some other geopolitical zones which have cultural affinity with the people of the south-east zone are introducing the diarchy system of governance in their communities.

[3] In Anambra state the monarchy and the town union are parallel, neither is under the other.

through group decision and did not respect centralized authority especially authority centralized on one personality. That served the people well when populations were low and it was possible for everybody to have a say and be heard directly, not through a representative, on community affairs. Beginning in the late 1950s emerging Igbo politicians in the Nigerian national context needed a new system that would help them mobilize consensus in the communities under increasing population and the traditional leadership arrangement, namely the monarchy that was already serving the rest of Nigeria was handy. But the British colonial government started this process earlier. When the British assumed control of Eastern Nigeria, the colonial officers appointed in each community someone they described as a paramount chief, a man through whom they governed the community[4].

The introduced governance structure did not expunge the arrangement that was indigenous to the people. Separately from the paramount chief, every Igbo community organized a town union without government influence as a platform for implementing self-help development projects and activities in their communities. In cities all over the world where members of an Igbo community had sufficient number of people they formed a branch of their town union for the purposes of supporting one another where they are and contributing toward the development of their home towns. Beginning in the 1990s, governments of the states of South-East geopolitical zone recognized the town union as a parallel part of the fourth tier administration in order to exploit the potentials of the indigenous system as a rural development oriented organization. The state governments moderate the governance of the town unions, especially with respect to the election of officers, a process which started to cause friction with the increasing importance of the organization. The state governments also recognize officially unarmed local police force called vigilante in each community.

The self-help community development service addressed in this book was performed in Anambra state in the South-East geopolitical zone (hereafter Eastern Nigeria). Anambra state has 23 Local Government Areas and 177 communities. The Ukpo Dunukofia (hereafter Ukpo) community in which the self-help development service was rendered is in

---

[4] A paramount chief was superior in authority to pre-existing leaders; the British colonial officers recognized that before their arrival there were leaders in each community.

Dunukofia Local Government Area. Ukpo is a town in transition from a rural village society to an urban community. The well-to-do minority live side by side with impoverished majority in the same neighborhoods. Most of the poor hardly know their rights and responsibilities in the community. Some members of the well to-to-do minority engage in token charity while ignoring social justice which is lacking in the society (Appendix IV). Needs for improvements in basic necessities of the people are monumental and the burden weighs heavily on the poor.

The community development service was provided on the platform of the Ukpo town union which was founded in 1944 and named Ukpo Improvement Union (UIU) by newly educated (at primary level) elites from the community who were few in number then[5]. The UIU maintained track roads as well as the village headwater in the community; provided structures for the village schools; constructed a post office, a maternity home (now the Nnamdi Azikiwe University Teaching hospital), etc.; and routinely organized entertainments at Christmas. Members of the community residing at home and abroad contributed money, materials, and direct labor for those initiatives. Women maintained sanitation by periodically sweeping and removing garbage from public spaces such as the village market square and other places of community gatherings. Later the UIU established secondary schools, sunk a community water borehole and laid pipe throughout the town. The water system did not function because the UIU lacked the financial and managerial resources to sustain it.

The present UIU constitution was written in 1999. The constitution provides for branches to be formed in cities and locations outside the town. It also provides for wings such as Women wing, Student wing, etc. The branches and the wings are under the Central Executive of UIU which is *the* UIU. A Central Executive of the UIU has three year tenure and it is composed of twelve elected members that include the President General, the overall head of the UIU and a pivotal position. The position of the President General could be part time or full time depending on the incumbent. But none of the positions including the position of the President General is remunerated.

Elected leaders of the four villages that make up the Ukpo town, namely Oranto, Isiekwulu, Akpu, and Akaezi are also members of the

---

[5] History of Ukpo Improvement Union by Eric Omejilichi, unpublished.

Central Executive. Of these four villages, Akaezi is the smallest by a large margin in terms of population and it is the home village of this author. The twelve positions of the Central Executive of the UIU that are filled with elected members including that of the President General are grouped into four and the groups rotate among the four villages every three years when a new UIU is formed. In the Ukpo community the monarchy consists of the monarch referred to as "Igwe" and his cabinet called "Igwe-in-Council". Membership of the cabinet is by appointment by the monarch and all the positions and memberships of the monarchy institution are for lifetime.

In 2006, it was the turn of Akaezi village to elect the President General to head the UIU for the following three years. This author was invited by the people of the Akaezi village to provide the leadership of the UIU on their behalf for the period 2006 to 2008. In his 2008 President General address at Ofala festival in the town, the author explained that his decision to return to his village from his base and work in the United States to answer the call from home to serve was rooted on two compelling factors (Appendix V)[6]. One factor was the death of two leaders, Edwin Nweke and Patrick Okoye around whom political, economic and social lives of the people of Akaezi village revolved and a third death, namely that of Christopher Nwafor who would have been a more appropriate candidate than the author of this book to serve as the President General on behalf of Akaezi village[7]. The sudden and unexpected deaths in quick succession of the three personalities left the Akaezi people bereft and in state of confusion and hopelessness.

The other compelling factor was the need to give back for the fortune of the author's life for which Ukpo prepared him. He belonged to the generation that took a child's growth and development as a collective Ukpo responsibility. Any adult had the right to call to order a child acting in socially unaccepted manner. A hungry child could eat just by waiting for food to be ready in any nearby kitchen. The author's formative primary education was dual: literacy and Christian religious

---

[6] In Anambra state, traditional leaders of the 177 communities celebrate what is known as Ofala festival on different dates each year. But because of the enormous cost of the festival only a handful of traditional leaders, including the traditional leader of Ukpo has continued the practice on a yearly basis. In Ukpo, the Ofala festival is celebrated on the last Saturday before Christmas each year.

[7] Christopher Nwafor died in 2002 just before his retirement was due. He worked as an Engineer at the Nigerian Airways Authority.

morals. Through these, several Ukpo people had profound influence on him and these were strong in shaping his life.

Ukpo town center known as Oye market square is at N 06"11.761' and E 06"58.320'. Oye is the second day of the indigenous four day week among the Igbo people. In the past, market was held on Oye day in the Oye market square once in four days. But as the society transitions to urban community, Oye market has become a daily market. The Oye market square is also used as a place of gathering for community wide events such as meetings and festivals. The Enugu-Onitsha express way which was opened in 1979 passes through the town.

The people of Ukpo community are heathens but most are incongruously Christians at the same time. The word heathen is commonly used to refer to a person that does not acknowledge the God of Christianity, Judaism or Islam. Most of the people of Ukpo overtly acknowledge the God of Christianity and covertly perform heathen rites. The current population of Ukpo is not known because the result of the latest population census in Nigeria that was conducted in the year 2006 is not published at the community level. But the voter registration conducted in Nigeria in 2007 returned more than 22,000 as the number of people in Ukpo who were aged eighteen years and above and therefore, was qualified to vote[8].

For clarity, the Central Executive or the UIU reported in this book is referred to as the town union government. President General without qualification is used to refer to the President General during the tenure of the UIU and that is the author. All other president generals are qualified with the dates of their tenure such as President General 2000 to 2002. In Anambra state, the term "Igwe" is used to refer to the traditional head of a community. For the purpose of general readership, the term "traditional leader" is used in place of Igwe[9]. Use of names of people and places is reduced to a minimum for the benefit of a wider audience. Individuals are referred to by their positions in the community with the exceptions of two personalities, namely Walter Eze and his brother, Arthur. The reason for the exceptions is that the contributions

---

[8] Delimitation of Federal Constituencies: Situating Dunukofia Local Government Area to the Chairman Independent National Electoral Commission, Abuja, 18th July 2008. R. C. Eze.

[9] Dr. Robert C. Eze was the traditional leader (the "Igwe") of Ukpo during the tenure of the UIU of 2006 to 2008.

of the two individuals toward the development of the Ukpo community are exceptional.

This book is in eleven chapters: the first Chapter is on fund raising activities. Interventions by the town union government are discussed in Chapters 2 to 6. The role of gender in the community service is discussed in Chapter 7 under collaboration with external bodies which was led by a woman. The differing roles that faith played in the community service are synthesized in Chapter 8. The leadership style which led to accomplishments of the town union government is discussed in Chapter 9. In Chapter 10 the important issue of sustainability of the interventions is analyzed and the book is summarized in the final chapter.

In the Ukpo community a president general is required to present an address on the state of the community in form of a report on the activities of the town union and major events in the community in the passing year. The addresses by the author as the President General for the three years, 2006 to 2008 are attached as appendices in this book. The President General's inaugural address and his address to a joint meeting of the cabinet of the traditional leader and the town union on the subject of "Mutual Respect among Leadership Institutions in Ukpo" are also attached as appendices.

CHAPTER ONE

Resource Mobilization

From the onset, it was clear that the level of financial resources it could generate would determine the performance of the incoming town union government. Only a few of the problems of the community could be solved without money; most would require large amounts of money. On the other hand, at that time state government did not subvent town unions which are considered as self-help voluntary organizations because of their origin.

Members of the Ukpo community were required by town union governments to pay an annual security levy of 1200 Naira per person[10]. Although that was a small amount most people did not pay. To enforce payment, the previous town union government introduced a measure that made it impossible for a family whose member owed the fee to celebrate in the town any event, such as marriages and funerals that required participation of members of the community. The measure involved posting a flag at the event venue entrance; the flag is red as a warning for people not to enter or green as a sign that the coast is clear. Yet, the amount generated from that source was too small to impact on the annual financial needs of the various town union governments. People paid only when they needed community members to participate in their events. The previous town union government depended more on voluntary contributions for about eight million Naira it raised in its three year tenure.

During the holiday season of December 2005 when many members of Ukpo community would have been at home for Christmas, the President General designate, before his inauguration on December 29 of that year went round visiting selected members of the community to solicit pledges of support in terms of money, ideas and services in kind. Choice of people to solicit those pledges from was based on subjective estimates of wealth of money, wealth of ideas and disposition for community service. Public display of wealth as exhibited in the size of

---

[10] 16 Naira was equivalent to US$1.00 at that time

houses was seen as a good approximation of the people's level of income.

In the round of visits, ideas that would later be handy to the town union government flowed and pledges of in-kind support in terms of services were numerous. But the visits revealed that money would not be easy to generate. Several of the people that owned big houses in the community complained of business setback. Commonly, with the initial money they earn people build big houses in the village to show evidence of success. Such people fail to reinvest in their businesses. As a result their businesses do not grow and the individuals do not continue to earn increasing amounts of incomes at the later stages in their lives when family needs for money are increasing with expanding family size. But such people continue to be seen as well-to-do in the community because of their big houses.

Towards the end of its term of office, the outgoing town union government produced a plan for revenue generation through what it described as Graded General Levy[11]. Some of the people visited favored this plan in preference to voluntary contributions. In the context of Ukpo community, fund raising by compulsory levy is problematic in many respects. There are no identities of the people of Ukpo origin who would qualify to be levied; no statistics of their income status; or even their location of abode, many lived outside the community, some outside Nigeria. Apart from this, collection of compulsory levies would be a complex effort because such levies are comparable to government taxes which most people do not pay without some form of coercion.

The people who favored levies proposed two alternative strategies to enforce payment, namely ostracism of defaulters or confiscation of their property. Neither of these alternatives was feasible in the context of the community. Ostracism amounts to denial of individual rights which is illegal under Nigerian law. Besides, ostracism is ineffective under circumstances of many defaulters. In the particular case of payment of compulsory levies in the community defaulters can easily outnumber compliers.

---

[11] Secure Your Fatherland and be Counted Addressed to Prof Felix Nweke on August 25, 2005 by R. C. Eze and G. E. Okeke.

The alternative of confiscation of property would not be less of a challenge. People who proposed this strategy made reference to the past when the strategy worked. In the past the community was a small and simple society; most members lived in the community; and people were relatively ignorant of their constitutional rights. Besides, amounts of levies were low and could be covered with a confiscation of simple personal belongings such as a goat or a bicycle. But times have changed; the population is now large and more sophisticated with relatively high levels of awareness of individual rights. Confiscation can be interpreted as a break-in with implication for litigations. The amounts of money being levied are large and in many cases the value of household belongings may not cover them. Confiscation of belongings of people who reside outside the community such as urban centers and foreign countries would be almost impossible.

On January 1, 2006 the Ukpo Security Council met to deliberate on the crucial matter of raising funds necessary for pursuing land cases with two neighboring communities pending in courts[12]. The incoming President General in his maiden address at his inauguration three days earlier on December 29, 2005 had declared the two land cases as the number one priority of the incoming town union government (Appendix I). Among issues discussed at the Security Council meeting were the establishment of a Security Council Finance Committee to help raise money for the town union government and the fund raising approach.

The incoming President General rejected out rightly the establishment of Security Council Finance Committee on the grounds that the function of the committee would erode the independence of the town union government and make the town union subordinate to the Security Council. The incoming President General insisted on fund raising through voluntary contribution arguing that in addition to the well-known implementation difficulties of compulsory levy, the approach had potential to create tensions and conflicts in the community and could produce unpleasant consequences at a time the community was at legal wars in two fronts. Members of the council grudgingly acquiesced on both issues since the incoming President General would head the town union government and lead the fund raising implementation. The

---

[12] Ukpo Security Council was constituted as an ad-hoc committee to manage the land litigations between Ukpo and two neighboring communities, respectively.

acquiescence, particularly in the case of voluntary contribution approach was grudging because several prominent members of the council continued after the meeting to agitate for fund raising through compulsory levy[13].

Members of the community received the news of the fund raising plan of voluntary contribution with both cheer and apprehension. The people had been anxious in waiting to know how the new President General would finance his expensive priority project, namely the two land cases. The masses of the people cheered the fund raising plan by voluntary contribution. Compulsory levy would have meant considerable financial burden for many. But some members of the community feared that voluntary contribution would not generate sufficient money to finance the land litigations in which case the result would be catastrophic.

On January 2, 2006, a day after the Security Council meeting two people brought checks of 500,000 Naira each and subsequently donations poured in, literarily. The President General engaged on fundraising tour of the branches of the town union government in different cities and locations beginning with North American branch from which he returned with a generous amount of money. At the same time the President General continued his appeal by visiting individuals at home and in Onitsha, a nearby city with a large concentration of successful businessmen of Ukpo origin. Need for money for the land cases often arose on short notice. Such money could be raised timely only from community members who lived nearby. There were a few of the community members at home and in nearby towns who responded with donations almost as many times as they were approached.

About the middle of the first year, i.e. 2006, the town union government had raised eight million Naira and by the end of its tenure in December 2008 nearly seventy million Naira[14]. The successful fund raising turn out stood on two strategies and providence. Periodic circulation of income account with list of contributors inspired donations. Members of the community applauded generous donors who became heroes of the community causes, especially the land cases that

---

13 [Ukpo Forum] Property Development in Ukpo addressed to My Dear Townsfolks on October 9, 2007 by KanayoEjem.

14 Ukpo individual contributions, 2006 to 2008 and Jan to July 8, 2009.

were overriding in importance to the community. In the Nigerian context, expenditure accounts are usually not trusted. In the country, printed receipt is not common and hand written receipt is issued mostly on demand. When asked for the business agent may write the receipt or issue a blank letter headed receipt paper to the client to write to his satisfaction.

Typical residence of a few well-to-do members of the Ukpo community. Courtesy: Regency Photos.

The President General leading by example was also an effective strategy; he made the second highest donation though by a wide margin behind the largest donor. But providence also favored the town union at the time. One individual, a wealthy member of the community, Arthur Eze who is a member of Fortune 500 was the largest contributor with close to half of the total amount generated in the three years of the town union government, not counting considerable amounts the patriot spent directly on various causes of the community. Arthur Eze wrote checks to the town union government frequently, in each occasion after reviewing the list of voluntary contributors with satisfaction.

There were challenges. Certain prominent members of the community argued that since Ukpo had good defenses in both land litigations huge expenditures were not necessary. Certain other members queried payments to lawyers arguing that some payments did not return commensurate value for money and used one case to illustrate their point. One lawsuit one of the two teams of lawyers was paid to prepare was muddled resulting in loss to the community in court. The same team of lawyers was paid again to return to the court to correct the error. No doubt, in a civilized society these arguments are correct. But in the Nigerian context a good defense does not necessarily translate into justice because of the prevalence of corruption in the judiciary. In dealing with lawyers in Nigeria especially on important matters like land cases one has to tread with prudence. Lawyers sometimes engage in double dealings. A lawyer can take money from opponent to betray his client. Ukpo was lucky with her teams of lawyers. The leaders of the teams handled both land cases from their inceptions and there was no instance of betrayal.

Typical residence of the masses of members of the Ukpo community. Courtesy: Regency Photos.

Looking ahead, there will be need to devise a continuous revenue generation strategy while preserving the self-help principle on which the town union institution was founded. Since 2012 the town union government is funded almost exclusively by one community member, namely Arthur Eze, obviously an unsustainable arrangement. In spite of its shortcomings, the voluntary contribution approach served well under what could be described as emergency situation, namely the land litigations. The approach should be part of a future strategy but alone it is not sustainable over time because donor fatigue was evident after a while during the emergency period. The Graded General Levy plan of the previous town union government did not specify whether the compulsory contribution is periodic or once in the lifetime of an individual community member.

The town union government of 2006 to 2008, i.e. the town union government under discussion, towards the end of its three year term sought to introduce property development and sales taxes, a version of the graded levy approach that would be on-going and targeted to people presumed to have the ability to pay. The large sum of money that the town union government raised in its three year tenure under the voluntary contribution approach was donated by only eight-five members out of the entire population of the community. Yet during the same period the number of individuals who were setting up expensive large buildings in the town was high. The town union government did not have time to implement the community bylaw. Besides, several members of the community frowned at the measure arguing that it is a partisan law because it targets people who are developing property or transacting in property[15].

The town union government of 2009 to 2011 considered business taxation but did not complete the census of businesses needed to establish the necessary statistics. As the urbanization of the community progresses businesses are growing in numbers. The transportation industry is a case in point. Different types of taxis including motorcycle taxis are conveying people to and from places of work in public and private sectors in the community. This is a departure from the past when work places were mostly nearby gardens and small farms to and from

---

[15] [Ukpo Forum] Property Development in Ukpo addressed to My Dear Townsfolks on October 9, 2007 by Kanayo Ejem.

which people commuted on foot. Apart from the transport related businesses, there are numerous other businesses that serve the growing population of the community that is undergoing rapid urbanization. The business taxation option should be pursued bearing in mind that the town union is a traditional organization that does not have experience in collecting and accounting for small amounts of money paid by large numbers of individuals.

The challenge is to balance the self-help element with demands of urbanization that include expanded responsibilities and therefore increased budget needs of the town union. Some communities in Anambra state have advanced further than Ukpo in the process of transition to urban communities. Ukpo community is situated between Awka and Onitsha, two urban centers which were traditional village communities that transformed into major metropolitan cities and still maintain the diarchy form of community governance. The experiences of the two hitherto traditional but now urban communities should be studied by the town union organization in Ukpo for lessons in revenue generation they may offer.

To summarize, the town union government was successful with mobilizing funds through voluntary contributions by members of the community to finance its priority projects, namely land cases in court with two neighboring communities. Much success was achieved because members of the community saw victories in both court cases as imperative; there was openness in handling the town union government finances; the President General led by example by making substantial donation; and because of the exceptional patriotism shown by a wealthy member of the community. But to continue to finance its development activities as a self-help organization in the community the town union has to devise a strategy for fund raising on an on-going basis.

CHAPTER TWO

Conflict Resolution

Disagreement over property ownership, called land dispute in the area, is the most common source of tension. The conflicts that are generated by intensified demographic and market pressures on land are common between families and between communities. In the past, land had limited market value; in most places, farmland was neither sold nor purchased. Unoccupied land in residential areas could be used as collateral for village moneylender loans. The lender had use right over the land until the borrower was able to repay the loan, which in some cases never happened. With population pressure on land, surviving members of families of borrowers sought to recover the land which their progenitors used as collateral for long standing loans. Resistance by survivors of the lending families who in some cases would not realize that the parcels of land did not belong to their families resulted in conflict. The town union government shied away from handling family conflicts because of their large numbers and focused on conflicts with neighboring communities, namely Abba and Abagana.

Communities are usually separated by broad areas of open spaces described as farmland. Boundaries are either not defined or based on land marks such as water ways. Where clear land mark did not exist communities based boundaries on where members cultivated. Patches of such land were randomly cultivated under extended fallow periods or shifting cultivation. In the past, immigrant communities were permitted to establish settlements in the unused open spaces with defined limits of access.

But population and commerce have grown rapidly in the area. For example, the population of Dunukofia Local Government Area increased by 50 percent within a period of fifteen years from 64,106 in 1991 to 96,517 in 2006. The first motorable road in Ukpo community was opened in 1925 and it was a dirt road[16]. By the end of 2000s, there

---

[16] This is the Otimgbodomgbo road which links the old Enugu-Onitsha road to the new Enugu-Onitsha dual carriage way.

were two tarmacked roads linking various other communities to the Enugu-Onitsha express way that was opened in 1979 through the town[17].

The pressure from growths in population and commercial activities resulted in land use intensification and communities began laying claim of ownership to open land spaces. A conflict erupted between Ukwulu and Abba communities both of which share boundaries with Ukpo. Abba, said to be an immigrant community in the area, crossed the water way that marked the land mass allowed their progenitors and claimed ownership of the entire area of land between Ukwulu and Ukpo including part of Ukpo land mass[18]. In 1975 the matter went to court and Ukpo people gave evidence in the court to the effect that Abba people went beyond the area of land allowed their progenitors[19].In 1985 Abba joined the Ukpo community in the case.

The court case lingered and because Ukpo people insisted on legal solution Ukwulu people who would rather resort to violence took a sideline position. In 1999 the court ruled in favor of Ukpo and Ukwulu. Abba people appealed against the 1999 judgment and requested the court for stay of execution of the judgment pending the determination of their appeal. In the year 2000, the court granted the request for the stay of execution of the 1999 judgment and ruled that all the parties were bound to maintain peace in the area of the disputed land pending the determination of the appeal filed by the Abba people in 1999[20]. The Abba people engaged in a loud celebration of this injustice against Ukpo with burn fires and provocative songs that were directed to the people of Ukpo community.

---

[17] Access road is often used by Economists as an index of level of commercialization. Enugu was the administrative capital of Eastern Nigeria and Onitsha which is less than 25 kilometers away from Ukpo was the largest commercial center in Eastern Nigeria.

[18] "Abba town in Njikoka Local Government is said to have been established by Ichida warriors who were assisting their brothers of Adazinnukwu against Nise people. Some of the warriors, who were cut off behind the enemy line, found their way to the present location of Abba town where they settled" (Ezebube 1992, p. 42).

[19] In the Supreme Court of Nigeria Holden at Abuja, Suit Nos. AA/53/75 and AA/11/77 (Consolidated), Appeal No. CA/E/161M/2004 SC/104/2005. Plaintiffs/Respondents' on Motion Dated 3/6/05 and Filed on 7/6/05. Dated this 23rd day of May 2006.By WoleOlanipeku (for).

[20] The Time for Intervention is Now by The Concerned Citizens of Ukpo

As the stay of execution was unconditional it granted to the Abba people what they could not secure in the substantive suit as evacuation of the stay of execution depended on hearing of the appeal that they filed which was up to them not to press for. They lost interest in their appeal. It took the court four years, 1999 to 2003 after the appeal was filed by the Abba people in 1999 to invite the parties in the suit for settlement of records of appeal, which in normal circumstances should have been done within six months. After the settlement of records of appeal in 2003 Ukpo people again waited until 2005 for the hearing of the appeal to commence. Then another absurd thing happened! The court declared that the record of proceedings of the 1999 judgment was missing. With that, the Abba people appealed for retrial of the 1999 judgment. But there was no accident such as fire in the court, no natural disaster or civil disturbance in the area that could have led to the loss of such a vital court document. Ukpo people were in dilemma.

Eugene Otunabo was a prime witness in the Ukpo-Abba land dispute. Courtesy: Eugene Oiunabo.

31

Abagana embraced development earlier than all the neighboring communities including the Ukpo community. A colonial settlement was established in the Abagana community early though later moved to another community. In 1910, the British colonial government established a court and in 1912 the Anglican community established church and school in Abagana. What is now old Enugu-Onitsha road was opened through Abagana and tarmacked since the mid-1940s. The result is that Abagana people went to school (primary) earlier than people in the neighboring communities and worked as domestic servants for British colonial officers, occupied positons in the colonial government as messengers, etc. and went on to occupy senior administrative positions in Nigerian governments at the dawn of independence.

In 1982, the Abagana people in senior positions in Anambra state government surreptitiously registered as their own the Ukpo part of the land that separates the two communities and planned to build a housing estate in their name in the property. In 1995 after the mischief leaked Ukpo people sued the Abagana people to court and the case also lingered[21]. The Ukpo people became psychologically fatigued by the injustice of the unconditional stay of execution of the 1999 judgment in their favor in the dispute with Abba people; by the Abagana people's ploy; and by the loss of their leader, Dr. Walter Eze who died unexpectedly in 1991. The need to re-energize the people was palpable.

On 29 December 2005, the incoming town union government announced the reactivation of the two court cases as a priority and reaffirmed commitment to a legal solution (Appendices I and III). Violence that will result in bloodshed will make peace difficult to negotiate after victory is won and without peace the victory will be lost. For their stand on non-violent solution the leaders of the Ukpo community found supportive strength in the faith of the people of the community in a god that forbids bloodshed by an Ukpo indigene on Ukpo soil.

The incoming town union government called on the people of Ukpo to wake up from despondence with a reminder of the high costs of yielding to fatigue. The humiliation of losing their birth right to land to an immigrant community would hunt generations of Ukpo people for a

---

[21] In the High Court of Anambra State of Nigeria, In the High Court of Otuocha Judicial Division Holden at Otuocha Before His Lordship Hon. Justice V. N. Umeh on Wednesday the 16th of November 2011. Suit No. A/174/1995.Judgment Order by Obadiegwu, D. M.

long time to come. Ukpo would be landlocked between Abba and Abagana communities without land link to Awkuzu, Ukwulu, Enuguagidi and Enugwu-Ukwu. Abba and Abagana will achieve their common desire of being joined by a land mass to proof their relationship as common descendants of Owele ancestry which Abba people desperately need to deny their immigrant status[22].

The incoming town union government assured Ukpo community that justice being delayed would ultimately be secured provided that the people rose up to their responsibilities. Contribution of money was the most important of such responsibilities. In Nigeria, court cases, especially inter community land cases, are quite expensive and convoluted as is illustrated by the drama being played out by the judiciary in the Ukpo-Abba case. Members of the judiciary, both the bar and the bench appear to lack interest in bringing land cases to closure and seem to revel in delays. They engage in frequent court adjournments and reschedules for reasons that may not be appreciated by laymen. Preparations by parties to a case for a scheduled court sitting include payments that are non-refundable if the sitting fails to hold. The payments must be repeated in subsequent schedules.

The incoming town union government policy of voluntary contribution of money turned out to be the impetus the people of the community needed to contribute towards the struggle. If wealthy people were allowed to get away with payment of the Graded General Levies which ranged from 3,000 to 500,000 Naira each based on presumed individual incomes as was proposed by the previous town union government, the amount of money required to execute the two court cases would not be raised[23]. The reason is that a sufficient number of the presumed well-to-do people would not pay at the higher levels of the levy. But the voluntary contribution policy made it possible for some people to donate large sums of money. Some people donated amounts that were several times the maximum they were required to pay as levy[24]. People who did not have money could contribute in other ways such as

[22] A close English translation of the Igbo word "owele" is backyard. Descendants of Owele ancestry, i.e. "Umu Owele" in Igbo are descendants of people who entered through the backyard.

[23] US$1=166 Naira.

[24] Ukpo individual contributions, 2006 to 2008 and Jan to July 8, 2009.

33

ideas and personal appearance in court at sittings either in the witness box or mere presence as a morale booster for lawyers and witnesses.

People were galvanized and enthusiasm electrified. Buoyed by the town union government approach to financial openness of periodically making the list of contributors available to the public, money by voluntary contributions poured in. Ideas in terms of suggestions to the town union government of what to do also flowed in and the cases became subjects of discussions in social gatherings. Optimism was in the air in spite of the rampant adjournments of court sittings on the cases.

Samuel Ugoezue was a prime witness in the Ukpo-Abagana land dispute. Courtesy: Samuel Ugoezue.

One of the ideas that were proffered was that Ukpo people should appeal to the Nigerian National Human Rights Commission for redress of the injustice of the missing court proceedings that enabled Abba people to appeal for retrial of the 1999 judgment that was in favor of Ukpo people. The National Human Rights Commission ordered the Anambra state judiciary to investigate the matter. The commission of enquiry set up by the Anambra state judiciary to investigate the matter decisively traced the document to the desk of a clerk of the court. With this the court denied the plea by Abba people for retrial of the 1999 judgment and removed the unconditional stay of execution of the same judgment. In 2011 a state high court ruled on the Ukpo-Abagana case in favor of Ukpo and the Supreme Court of Nigeria ruled the Ukpo-Abba case also in favor of Ukpo. Excitement reigned among the people of Ukpo but the leaders of the community always conscious of the need for peace after victory counselled against loud celebrations that could pass a sense of mortification to the opponents and jeopardize peace negotiations later. Following that the celebration of the victories by the people of the Ukpo community was in form of sober reflections through speeches in which people who labored for the justice some of whom were already dead were remembered. The opponents were hailed for their formidable defense in court without violence and they were invited to negotiate peace.

During the period of the court cases between Ukpo and Abagana and between Ukpo and Abba Ukpo leaders were inundated with propositions and counsels on what to and what not to do by well-meaning members of the Ukpo community who were nervous in anticipating the final outcomes. The people of Ukpo community saw the conflicts as determinants of their existence as a community. Abba people were highly provocative in two ways that were aimed at spurring Ukpo people to physical and spiritual war fares. They continuously acted with latitude by erecting structures and billboards of their names in the disputed area. Several Ukpo people especially young people pushed in support of responding to the provocations towards violence while others cautioned against it. Ukpo leaders stood firm against violence and found ally in the Ukpo people's faith in a non-violence god.

Second, Abba people frequently placed odd objects with diabolic intentions at strategic positions in Ukpo by night when their agents would not be noticed and in court premises on sitting days. Some of the objects were supposed to cause deaths of prominent Ukpo people and others to create confusion in the minds of Ukpo witnesses and lawyers in the court. Some Ukpo people had ideas of superior means of spiritual warfare and advised that the approach be pursued. This approach was easily ignored because Ukpo leaders did not believe in its efficacy. Even if it were to be effective the approach will be a violation of the non-violence position of the Ukpo leaders.

Different people in Ukpo knew lawyers that would enhance the strength of the existing teams and some knew other lawyers that would outperform the teams. One community member offered to pay 10 million Naira to an influential lawyer to take over from an existing team[25]. These and other proposals and offers with respect to lawyers were more difficult to ignore. In case of undesirable outcome of loss in either conflict the blame will be unbearable. Because of that more lawyers were engaged to strengthen the existing teams. But after a considerable amount of money was spent it became clear that the added lawyers did not contribute much to the impact and they were dropped. The initial teams of lawyers competently, patiently, and loyally carried on to the end and their efforts were rewarded with successes in both cases.

Fettish objects like this one were commonly placed with diabolic intentions by opponents in land disputes at locations in Ukpo at nights and in court premises on sitting days. Courtesy: Eugene Otunabo.

The role of the traditional leader of the Ukpo community was central to the success of the conflicts resolution effort. His position on non-

---

[25] One team of lawyers for Ukpo-Abba case and one for Ukpo-Abagana case.

violence was resolute. He frequently made reference to a similar case elsewhere that seems endless because instead of the substantive land suit the court is focusing on numerous cases of murder and arson that resulted from violence. The violence in that case was provoked by the side to the conflict whose case is weak intentionally to prolong the substantive suit. The traditional leader was a connoisseur in the oral history of the area; his grandfather was the paramount chief that the British colonial officers appointed for Ukpo; his father and senior brother respectively were traditional leaders of the community before him; and he is resident in the community for almost all his life. He provided a historical account of the area which left no one in Ukpo in doubt that pursuing both conflicts was a just cause. He was able to mobilize and motivate the right people as witnesses whose evidences in the courts were convincing. The wisdom he brought to the management of the conflicts communicates a consciousness that he was on a mission on behalf of the ancestors.

Some leaders of Ukpo community celebrate victory in the land dispute against Abba community with sober reflection under the cool shed of a tree. Courtesy: Regency Photos.

In summary, the conflicts between Ukpo community and two neighboring communities were both settled in favor of Ukpo in court without violence in spite of manipulations of justice over many years by the Nigerian judiciary and in spite of frequent provocations of physical and spiritual war fares by Abba people against Ukpo. The successes were achieved through the considerable sacrifice in terms of donations of money by some members of the community; by the determination of the people of Ukpo to pursue justice through legal rather than violent means; and by the competence and loyalty of the Ukpo teams of lawyers. The role of the traditional leader of the Ukpo community was central to the success of the effort. His historical account of the area, his unshakable position on non-violence, and his ability to mobilize and motivate convincing witnesses were indispensable for the successful resolution of the conflicts.

CHAPTER THREE

Cultural Revival

Traditional rites of passage, festivals of thanksgiving, and festivals of music and dance are among the cultural activities with which the people of Ukpo community are identified by the people of their neighboring communities. These activities are expressions of the people's religious orientations. The cultural activities were numerous in the past but they have been largely eroded by Christian civilization (Appendix IV). Some are no longer celebrated while some are celebrated with modifications to accommodate the Christian faith and in the process they have been stripped off their religious features. The latter are mainly those with parallels in the Western World. A few of the cultural activities are still celebrated with minimal or no modifications because of the continued potency of the heathen faiths in which they are grounded; these are principally rites of passage, namely marriage and funeral rites.

The coming of age rite of initiation of adolescents into manhood is an example of a cultural activity that is no longer celebrated. In the past, the celebration involved retreating of adolescent boys into a sacred forest where they underwent spiritual cleansing for 28 days at the end of which they emerged as adult men. This practice is reminiscent of the coming of age initiation ritual among the Xhosa people of South Africa. At adolescent, Xhosa boys retreat to the mountains for a period of one month during which they undergo circumcision and other initiation rites that are kept as secret to the uninitiated. At the end of the period the people descend from the mountains and are considered full grown men. The parallel in this practice between members of the Ukpo community who are Igbo people and the Xhosa people of South Africa is probably because the practices are of a common origin as both the Igbo and the Xhosa peoples are Bantus[26]. The Xhosa people sustained while the Igbo people of Ukpo failed to sustain the coming of age rite of initiation

---

[26] Nairaland: "Origin of the Bantu Peoples: Eastern Nigeria/Western Cameroun?" and Encarta dictionary.

probably because of the difference in the more recent history, in terms of colonization, of the two Bantu peoples[27].

Marriage and funeral rituals are rites of passage that are still celebrated. They are celebrated with little or no modifications by the Christian influence. These rites are respectively celebrated by all, twice by Christians first in a Christian way in the open and again in a heathen way most of the time behind closed doors or in the dark of the night to evade prying Christian priests. The rites are performed almost by all because they are individual activities that have deep spiritual significance and are seen by the people as imperative for their existence.

Traditional marriage rite is performed in all marriages with little or no modifications over time. It survived because of the traditional faith on which its potency is anchored. If not performed at the time of a marriage, it is performed retroactively if the marriage runs into a hitch or if a major sickness, death, or economic distress occurs in the family. If none of the mishaps is experienced the rites will still be performed retroactively before the marriage of a daughter born to the couple, even after the death of either or both of her parents.

Colorfully costumed women performing at the Opotor festival in February 2007. Courtesy: Regency Photos.

---

[27] Ukpo landscape was dominated by forests in the past; the landscape in the Eastern Cape Province of South Africa, home of the Xhosa people, is dominated by undulating hills.

Traditional funeral rites are also performed in all cases of death for both Christians and non-Christians because the traditional faith which gave rise to the rites has continued to haunt people who fail to perform them. Some Christians who act as if they do not have faith in the rites perform the ritual for their diseased relatives on the argument that the diseased relatives believed or the Christians will provide money to cover the expenses but say that they are not part of it.

Christians' pretentiousness about traditional funeral rites in Ukpo is better illustrated with true stories. Whether or not to perform the traditional funeral rite for a mother who died as a Christian, the Christian son sought advice from another Christian that was known to have sympathy for traditional religious practices who of course recommended the performance of the rite. The question to ask is why did the Christian son not ask his parish priest or why should he seek advice? If he did not believe or if he was not bothered he should have simply ignored the rite for his mother. Another Christian scheduled the funeral rite also for his mother and word got round to the parish priest. The Christian moved the venue of the rite elsewhere away from his home. On the scheduled day the priest came to his home early in the morning, stayed till late in the evening and left calling his informant a liar.

To determine someone's religious identity in Ukpo the correct question to ask is if the person is a Christian. In the community everybody is a heathen but most are also Christian in addition. Someone who does not confess the Christian, Jewish, or Moslem God is described as a heathen. The Christians in Ukpo confess the Christian God but do not honor the first of His commandments, namely "You shall have no other gods before me"[28].

Traditional festivals of thanksgiving and festivals of music and dance are communal events and the spiritual guilt for non-celebration does not weigh as heavily on an individual as in the cases of the rites of passage of marriage and funeral which are individual events. Because of this the traditional festivals of thanksgiving and of music and dance have suffered more onslaughts under the Christian overrun.

New Yam Festival is a thanksgiving event; it survived Christian invasion, though only partially. It is an agriculture related event that is

---

[28] The Holy Bible, New International Version. 1973, 1978, 1984 by International Bible Society. Exodus 20 page 56.

41

celebrated in September to mark the beginning of harvest season. In the past in Ukpo, New Yam Festival was celebrated with deep spiritual rites in form of gathering of extended family members to share meals and exchange gifts of yam and livestock and remember ancestors with gratitude in prayers. The New Yam Festival is still celebrated but without its original religious contents. The spiritual rites component of gathering of extended family members is now omitted by most people. Some people are no longer comfortable with sharing ritual meals with members of extended families composed of people of different faith, income class, and social status.

But even without the religious features, New Yam Festival remains immensely popular with the people of Ukpo. Every September during the festival period people of Ukpo origin return home in large numbers from different parts of Nigeria and some from outside the country to celebrate the festival. Gifts of livestock, money, and especially yam are still commonly exchanged among extended family members on both fathers' and mothers' sides. The festival partially survived the onslaught of Christianity because of its significance as a thanksgiving festival parallel to the popular North American Thanksgiving. Worldwide, different peoples celebrate nature's bounties in different ways and with different materials that are commonly available or are important in the history of the people. Ukpo is within the part of Eastern Nigeria that is considered by agricultural scientists as the place of origin of the white yam.

Opotor is a festival of music and dance in Ukpo; it is almost completely assailed by the Christian influence. Similar to New Yam Festival of thanksgiving Opotor festival of music and dance is an agricultural occasion that is held in February to mark the end of harvest and beginning of planting of crops. The Opotor festival is celebrated in a way that is reminiscent of North American Halloween including the early years of the Halloween festival in ancient Europe. The Opotor is a week-long festival; the celebration is both somber and cheerful. It begins with a six day prelude on Monday of its week and ends with a grand finale on Sunday. The six days of prelude are dominated by masked young men who prowl the streets and visit individual homes to collect gifts of money, yams and life chicken.

The Saturday night before the grand finale on Sunday is dominated by night masquerades which are heard but not seen. The provocative songs of the night masquerades are of both glee and grief and are aimed at helping people to deal with the mysteries, griefs and pains of life and death. For examples, the night masquerades in their songs remind people allegorically that man cannot engage gods in a war of revenge; that the brave who is killed in a family dispute is missed under external aggression; that if palm fruit is set deep in the tree long-billed birds are sought after at harvest time; etc. The masquerades resonantly extol Ukpo people dead and alive, who performed feats of courage on behalf of the community and ridicule others who are less courageous. The night masquerades call on certain living individuals with means to rise up to the challenges of the community.

Similar to Christmas songs, the songs of the night masquerades are seasonal used during the festival period but the magic of the songs lasts all year round. It is common to hear someone humming those songs any time. Whether in a moment of excitement or in a moment of despair, the night masquerades offer suitable songs to still the mind under any human condition. The grand finale is marked with all-day music and dance performances in the Oye market square by large numbers of scarily masked men and colorfully costumed women.

Each year people emerge from the Opotor festival with feelings of renewed physical and cleansed spiritual energies and are psychologically prepared for the next farming season that is imminent at the time of the festival. People who grow up in the community do not forget the inspirational thrill of the Opotor festival activities, songs and dances no matter where in the world such people may reside later in life. In that way, the cultural festival has the value of helping to keep the people mentally connected to their Ukpo roots.

In December 2007, a man of Ukpo origin who resides in the United States of America was home with his family for the holiday season. He proposed in a formal gathering in the community that the dates of the Opotor festival be shifted from February to between Christmas and New Year. The man who grew up in Ukpo would want his North American raised children and other children like them to be exposed to the spirit of the festival. That according to the man would help the children who are growing up in North America to maintain connection with their Ukpo roots.

The proposal was not discussed but it has merit. The Opotor festival is a traditional event; long ago when the dates were established to serve agricultural purpose farming was the occupation of everybody and virtually all lived in the community. Situation has changed; farming is no longer the occupation of most of the people and many community members who have interest in participating in the festival which now serves more than agricultural purpose reside outside the community.

The Opotor festival is losing popularity to Christmas, New Year, and Easter which are celebrated nationally in Nigeria partly because of its timing which is close to those of Christmas and New Year that compete for the interests of Ukpo people. After these two festivals that are constitutionally supported with national public holidays in Nigeria people are likely to be weary of celebrations, financially, physically, and psychologically. Most of the people who reside outside the community cannot afford to return home for Opotor in February soon after New Year in January.

A masked dancer performing at the Opotor festival of February 2007.
Courtesy: Regency Photos.

Intervention in the area of cultural revival during the tenure of the town union government from 2006 to 2008 was with respect to the revival of the Opotor festival that was carried out largely outside the context of the town union government. Certain members of the Central

Executive of the town union government considered that the Opotor festival should be revived because of its high social values. But in 2006 the Central Executive voted overwhelmingly against the town union involvement in organizing the festival except with providing security support during the festival[29]. The opposition argued that although the festival has high social values it is a heathen festival (Appendix IV).

Following the disappointing development, some members of the community immediately rallied round and constituted what they called "Forum for Promotion of Culture in Ukpo" to assume responsibility for reviving the festival and elected the President General as their patron. At the same time the President General in his personal capacity encouraged members of the community who did not acknowledge the God of Christianity to form an organization for group identity. The aims are to protect their religious interests under the increasing influence of Christianity and to help with the revival of heathen cultural activities including the Opotor festival of music and dance in the community.

The Forum for Promotion of Culture in Ukpo joined hands with the organized members of the people who do not confess the God of Christianity to promote the Opotor festival. Since then the festival has continued to be celebrated with its full heathen religious features. For example, before the week of the festival, the non-Christian group performs appeasement and petition rituals that are necessary to make the one week of celebration free of hazards that can arise out of excitement under conditions of large crowds. In addition, celebrants are encouraged to freely and openly pay homage to the matriarch god of the Opotor festival, a practice on which the Christians who were opposed to the festival based their argument that the festival is a heathen practice.

The Forum for Promotion of Culture in Ukpo introduced certain innovations in the celebration of the Opotor festival. For example, each year the forum extends formal invitations to the festival to leaders and performance troupes from several neighboring communities. Response to the invitations is always high both in terms of community leaders, performing troupes and spectators that attend each year from other communities. This gesture is important for enhancing cordial relationships with the neighboring communities.

---

[29] Motion Against UIU Taking a Leading Role in Opoto Festival 2008 addressed to PG and all members of the UIU Executive. January 23, 2008 by Nwachala Ifeaka E.

Since the Opotor festival was revived, there has been a turn-around on the part of the town union on its stance against the festival perhaps prodded by the traditional leader who is supportive of the festival promotion effort. For example, in 2013, the town union used the grand finale as the platform for inaugurating the President General of 2012 to 2014 that would have taken place on December 29, 2011 in another context. It was delayed because of problems associated with the election of the President General. In 2014, the town union contributed 400,000 Naira in support of the festival that year. That amount was about 55 percent of the total expenditure by the Forum for Promotion of Culture which was 750,000 Naira for the festival that year.

Arthur Eze, a wealthy philanthropist and a member of the Ukpo community addresses community members on Ukpo Day of December 2007. Courtesy: Regency Photos.

To summarize, traditional cultural activities in Ukpo suffered erosion by Christian influence. A traditional festival which competes with national festivals such as New Year, Easter, and Christmas needed promotion to survive the Christian overrun. During the tenure of the town union government from 2006 to 2008 the necessary promotion was provided outside the context of the town union by the Forum for Promotion of Culture in Ukpo in collaboration with the organization of non-Christians that was established by some members of the community. That was necessitated by a harsh opposition by some Christian members of the Central Executive against the town union involvement in the revival of the festival. But since then the town union has turned around to support the festival probably because of prodding by the traditional leader who is positive about the necessity to revive the festival.

A festival that has parallel in the western world, namely the New Yam Festival continues to be popular in the community; the festival survived the Christian influence partially. The festival is still popular but without its traditional religious features. Cultural rites of passage such as marriage and funeral rites survived the Christian invasion unscathed because they are individual spiritual activities that are anchored in heathen faiths that have continued to be potent. Double standards in Ukpo Christianity find expression in the imperative, for the existence of the people, of the traditional rites of passage. Virtually every member of the community engages, overtly or covertly, in the performance of the heathen rites of marriage and funeral.

CHAPTER FOUR

Environmental Protection

A culture of disrespect for the environment in terms of the practices of deforestation, noise pollution, and random waste (garbage, human and animal) disposal in the open was a serious matter calling for attention in the community by 2006. In the past, when population pressure on land was low, forestlands were protected as sacred spaces for traditional religious purposes. Some forestlands were revered as abodes of benevolent gods and served various spiritual purposes. For example, some sacred forests served as retreat grounds for passage rights such as initiation of adolescent boys into manhood. Some forests were feared as abodes of diabolic gods and were used as disposal grounds for bodies of people who died of diseases, such as swollen stomach, seen as divine curse. The same forests were also used as quarantine sites for people suffering major infectious and contagious diseases, such as leprosy and smallpox.

Christian religion and western education have conspired to erode the traditional need for protection of forestlands without presenting alternative solutions for the problem of environmental degradation under increased population pressure on land. Christian faith dispelled the fear of and reverence for sacred forests as superstition. Western education improved the understanding of causes and cures for many common health problems while some diseases such as smallpox have been eradicated and others such as leprosy are no longer common. With increased commercial activities and high population pressure on land in the absence of land use planning in the community forestlands are randomly cleared, farmed or built over either in full or partially. Large buildings and motorable roads that are increasing in numbers in the community mostly without drainage exacerbate gully erosion.

The population of Ukpo community appeared to have a high level of tolerance for noise. By 2006, loud noise was generated with electronic equipment during the day and night for a wide range of purposes including commercial advertisements, parties, public announcements, and above all Christian religious messages and services. Public announcements were by town criers using mobile electronic equipment through the town from mid-nights to early mornings when people were expected to be home. At parties such as funeral wake keeps music and speeches were broadcast so loud as if the purpose was to wake the dead.

But the nuisance effects of noise generated by churches exceeded that from all other sources combined. The churches were numerous and of varying congregation sizes. They were based everywhere including individual homes and no matter the size of the congregation, large or small, powerful electronic public address equipment with microphones mounted on roof tops or tree tops were used to announce their good messages, most of them all-night every night as if in competition for the loudest and most prolonged noise generator. To the people of the community all those appeared normal. Nobody seemed to notice the noise except in the cases of some churches that were based next door to people's homes. In the cases of such churches, the people were helpless. The people were afraid to incur the wrath of God or they had nowhere to lay their complaint since the churches belonged mostly to powerful people in the community.

Why was this degree of noise generated? Availability of relatively low cost electricity in the area remains a factor. Rural electrification began in the area in the mid-1960s. The use of generators facilitated by availability of petroleum fuel at relatively low cost cushioned off the effect of inefficiency in the rural electrification program of the government. Mass poverty, illiteracy and ignorance are contributory factors. Some mediums of mass communication such as radios and televisions are inaccessible to the masses because of wide spread poverty among the population. Print newspapers and leaflets are expensive to produce and distribute and not efficient among mostly illiterate population. Illiteracy, poverty, and insensitive governance in Nigeria render the masses ignorant of their constitutional rights. Under these circumstances, the use of electronic loud speakers is the most efficient in terms of private costs to the advertisers who can reach many people at a low private cost per person reached. But the social costs in terms of public health dangers are high.

Waste disposal practices in the community would produce a rude shock for someone from the western world who had no exposure to Africa. In Ukpo community garbage collection facility is rare whether in private homes or in public places. People randomly drop waste materials anywhere without a thought. The streets were dumping grounds for household, garden and business garbage. In two separate occasions during the tenure of the town union government from 2006 to 20008 garbage collection barrels were provided in the Oye market square, one by the Ukpo undergraduates students union and the other by the wealthy philanthropist, Arthur Eze. In both cases the facility was abused. The facility was not widely used because of the established habit of involuntary dropping of waste materials and because with time the much that was deposited in the barrels overflowed. Provision was not made for removal. The barrels eventually disappeared from the market square; they were carried away by people who had better uses for them.

Human waste disposal practices were more disgusting than garbage disposal practices. Men carelessly urinated in the open anywhere and whenever the need arose. A few households had pit latrines, fewer had water system, and still fewer could afford adequate supply of running water for flushing toilets. Large majority relied on the garden spaces and bushes around homes for stooling. Liquid waste from domestic washing and cooking water was channeled to the streets where almost as many sewage pools as there were homes were created. In the past unsanitary waste disposal practices were no big deal because there were relatively few people, open spaces were wide and garbage was degradable organic materials mostly. By 2006, population was high, open spaces were shrinking and garbage materials included metals, plastics and other non-degradable materials which continuously accumulated.

If not restrained, private interest exploits communal interest by transferring private costs to the community. Deforestation for private purposes, mass communication by means of electronic public address systems and random waste disposal practices have low private costs but their costs to the community are monumental. Ukpo is counted among several communities in Anambra state that are facing serious gully erosion problems which have claimed much land and threatens many homes. Cases of hypertension that could be linked to noise are common in the Nnamdi Azikiwe University Teaching hospital which serves people from Ukpo and neighboring communities.

Containing the flow of liquid wastes within the homestead boundary is inexpensive; it entails only a shallow pit. However, people find it cheaper to simply channel the liquid wastes into the streets with considerable costs, in terms of health hazard to the public. In Ukpo, diseases and deaths that result from the unhygienic living conditions such diarrhea and typhoid are frequently blamed by the people suffering them on some angry gods or on human enemies next door. Solutions are often sought in fetishism and traditional medicine that are more easily accessible and affordable to the poor than orthodox modern medicine.

Unhealthy social habits that are rooted in established culture can be corrected with efforts including relevant education programs and enforced legislation that are sustained over time. In 2006 the town union government could not engage in mass education that was capable of changing the established unhealthy cultural habits because the resources of the town union government in terms of both money and time were meagre. Instead, the town union government enacted bylaws to legislate against some of the cases of environmental abuse in the community and worked hard to enforce them with the hope that such effort would be sustained[30].

Enacting the bylaw against deforestation was problematic. Certain Christian members of the town union government opposed the law on the ground that, in their understanding heathen shrines could not be described as sacred. Because of their jealous God or out of ignorance those members denied the sanctity of the sacred spaces of their people (Appendix IV). Yet not only do every people have sacred spaces but also sacred days, sacred personalities, sacred meals, and sacred objects such as animals and plants. But the opposition which was on a subjective ground helped to extend the categories of sites to be protected as "public spaces, sites and forests" to include public squares that in the past served as gathering spaces for village meetings, marketing and for relaxation. Some of the public squares have survived encroachment though mostly partially.

Some community members suspected the town union of sinister motive with respect to the public space protection bylaw. The members suspected that the town union needed the spaces for public buildings such as town hall, health and education facilities. Although the spaces are for public use, some families are considered to be in charge of each space on behalf of the community. The suspicion was dispelled through vigorous campaigns in the community by members of the town union government.

The spaces as defined were identified, documented, and registered as public spaces in the community. The bylaw forbade removal, demolition or burning of any object in the public spaces without prior permission of the cabinet of the traditional leader. The cabinet should determine

---

[30] Ukpo Bylaws 2007, Ukpo Dunukofia.To Chairman Dunukofia Local Government. August 6, 2008. R. C. Eze and Felix Nweke.

appropriate penalty, depending on the extent of damage for default. The town union government appreciated the pre-eminence of protecting the public spaces and vested the enforcement of the bylaw in the cabinet for the purpose of sustainability[31]. The cabinet is a permanent community organization; each town union government had three year tenure. During the tenure of the town union government from 2006 to 2008 there was one case of default and the weight of the law was brought to bear with heavy penalty. Subsequently, the bylaw became popular and an effective deterrent to wanton deforestation.

Garbage regularly overflowed because provision was not made for removal. Courtesy: Regency Photos.

The bylaw against noise pollution banned operating electronic public address systems between the hours of 10.00 pm and 5.00 am within the boundaries of the community. The bylaw exempted the eves of community-wide festivals, namely New Year, Easter, Ofala, and Christmas that involved loud night entertainments. Penalty was impounding of the electronic public address equipment to be reclaimed

[31]UIU Resolutions: Conservation of Public Spaces. To the Secretary Igwe-in-Council. 24/05/07. NwachalaIfeaka.

on payment of N5,000[32]. The first defaulter was a town crier who made a public announcement during the forbidden hours with electronic public address system on behalf of a popular political party. The following morning the leader of the political party in the area attempted to intervene but was advised to pay the penalty and he did. There were a few more defaults and in each case the law was fully enforced. The bylaw became very popular. People who before appeared not to be bothered by loud noise applauded the law and some requested the town union government to extend the coverage to day time.

The town union government legislated against channeling of liquid waste to the streets and against the dumping of the garbage generated in the households, gardens and business premises in the streets. Penalty was low; N500 for default because virtually every household was a defaulter and most of them could not afford to pay more. For the wealthier members of the community who could afford to pay more the humiliation of having to pay fine, no matter how small would be sufficient deterrent. Street food vendors were required to clean up their spaces at the end of each business day or pay the same penalty.

Legislating against random dropping of garbage, urinating in the open, and stooling in the garden spaces and bushes around individual residences was not done because enforcement would require more resources for vigilance than available to the town union government. Legislating provision of toilet facilities in homes was prohibited by cost of the facilities to most community members. Most households could not afford pit latrines. There are places in Africa, such as Eastern Cape Province in South Africa where pit latrines are constructed for individual households by the local governments. The town union government did not have resources to do this for the households in the Ukpo community.

The town union government put measures in place to clean up the major roads and public squares in the community. This task appeared prohibitive because of garbage that piled up over time. Apart from the Enugu-Onitsha express road a five kilometer road was the only tarmacked road in the Ukpo community in 2006. The road was tarmacked in 2004 by the state government with shoddy drainage gutters.

---

[32] N166 =US$1.00.

Since it was tarmacked the road had not been cleaned[33]. The drainage gutters were filled up with garbage and sand and were overgrown with weed for the entire length of the road.

The town union government attempted to clean the road with voluntary communal labor by calling on the young men of the community to come out and help. The young men responded by coming out in large numbers but did little work and used the occasion as a social event. The town union government engaged some of the same young men as hired labor working daily for a week and used rented trucks to carry away the huge amounts of garbage, sand and weed that were dug up. After this initial cleaning, the town union government engaged two paid contractors to routinely clean the road and engaged a third contractor to also clean the Oye market square on continuous basis.

In summary, abuses of the environment were in various forms that included deforestation, noise pollution and various forms of unsanitary life styles. The abuses were intensified by increasing population and market pressures following the process of transition from rural to urban society. The town union was able to control the abuses to some extent by legislations. Legislation against deforestation was accomplished after overcoming rigid internal opposition within the town union government especially by certain Christian members who denied the sacredness of forestlands that served heathen purposes. Fears of sinister motive by some members of the community who thought that the town union was acquiring the spaces for public buildings also had to be dispelled before the legislation was enacted. But legislations against noise pollution and some forms of unsanitary practices sailed through the town union government with minimal opposition. The lesson is that people appreciate decency but need authority to enforce compliance.

The legislations were rigorously enforced. The enforcement was determined because defaulters included powerful members of the community such as well-to-do families especially in the cases of deforestation and unsanitary waste disposal practices. Defaulters also

---

[33] Has Otimgbodomgbo Road Become a Failed Contract and an Abandoned Project? To Governor Peter Obi, 28th August 2006.Felix Nweke and IfeakaNwachala.

Data Capture on the Present State of Dilapidation of the Road Linking KM0+000 Beginning from Oye-Agu Abagana up to K M4+960 at Ukpo Junction on the Enugu-Onitsha Expressway. 12th June 2006.

included church groups that used powerful electronic public address systems to broadcast their good messages.

CHAPTER FIVE

Interventions in Health and Education

At the inception of the town union government in 2006 there were three orthodox medical facilities in the Ukpo community. They included one health post where local government nursing assistants attend to patients three days in a week. The nursing assistants dispense pain killers free and advice patients with serious problems to go to hospitals, clinics or health centers for doctors' or nurses' attention. There was a health center with a resident midwife in the community also provided by the local government. The health center building was broken into two from the floor through the walls by an unidentified underground structural malfunction that threatened the building with collapse. Nnamdi Azikiwe University Teaching Hospital was also in place in Ukpo by 2006.

The Nnamdi Azikiwe University Teaching Hospital in Ukpo is a campus of the Nnamdi Azikiwe University's teaching hospital located some fifty kilometers away. The campus in Ukpo is the only hospital within a ten kilometer radius. A few true stories describe the sordid state of the hospital in 2006. A Michigan State University Teaching Hospital representative that came to evaluate the feasibility of student and faculty exchange programs between the two teaching hospitals was dismayed at the disreputable state of the Nnamdi Azikiwe University Teaching Hospital. The medical records were piled up in folders in the open covered over with considerable amount of dust that made one wonder how an individual's medical record could ever be found. The issue of privacy of such records did not matter. Out-patients used a narrow open space within the hospital premises for toilet facility. The Michigan State University representative did not want to continue the evaluation of the feasibility of the exchange programs but returned to the Michigan State University and wrote back that because of serious problems of insecurity in Eastern Nigeria the Michigan State University could not go ahead with the exchange plan.

An Ukpo community member reported to the town union government that the nurses at the Nnamdi Azikiwe University Teaching Hospital would not dress his ulcer sore because they found him smelly. The President General led a protest team of members of the town union government to the hospital; there more stories emerged. For example, not too long earlier an accident victim that was brought to the hospital was left to bleed to death unattended on the bare floor of the hospital building veranda because the doctor was not available to approve his admission. First aid was not administered on him; the nurses would not be bothered. A member of the town union government protest team wondered why people who are nurses by choice should be so unsympathetic. The resident medical doctor in charge of the hospital who did not deny any of the stories was not certain that the people trained as nurses by desire.

In Nigeria, several people enroll in nursing schools when they cannot get into professions of their choice such as medicine and pharmacy either because of lack of qualification or because of inability to pay training expenses. In Nigeria nursing schools are easy to get into because there are many of them providing training at different levels and of varying qualities and the programs are in most cases subsidized by government. Additionally, personnel in Nigerian hospitals are usually overworked with long hours and low pay and they have insufficient supplies and equipment for their work. Because of these shortcomings nurses who are stressed tend to transfer their frustrations on their patients.

In a neighboring community there are a few one doctor one nurse clinics with in-patient facilities. The clinics prescribe medicine and administer injection but refer serious cases to bigger hospitals in the area including the Nnamdi Azikiwe University Teaching Hospital. But there were cases of patients on admission at the Nnamdi Azikiwe University Teaching Hospital that moved over to the clinics for what they considered better attention.

Often, patients seek treatment in the orthodox facilities after they had tried and failed to recover through alternative treatment. All over Nigeria, both in rural and urban centers there are numerous one man medicine stores that illegally dispense medicines including injections at will to people. Most of such operators do not complete primary education. Their only training is as apprentices in the medicine stores of equally untrained medicine dealers. Ukpo has its share of such medicine stores and members of the community patronize them because they are relatively inexpensive and conveniently located and they provide immediate attention with politeness which are lacking in most of the orthodox facilities.

But fetish and traditional herbal medicine are by far the most common treatments for sicknesses in the community. Unrelenting headache or fever is usually attributed to malaria. The patient would collect herbs from the bush or buy them from one of several local medicine men who cannot diagnose but have medicine for virtually all ailments. For more serious cases, patients seek help from seers who are able to identify the god or a human enemy that is causing the sickness. The seers are also able to prescribe the type of appeasement or petition to the gods or what to do about the human enemy in order to be relieved.

Under these circumstances, what could the town union government do to bring about improvement in the health conditions of the people in the community? The interventions the town union government made to curtail the wanton abuses of the environment especially with respect to the unhygienic living style and noise pollution have a high potential to improve the health status of the people. This is because the common ailments such as diarrhea, tuberculosis, typhoid and hepatitis are traceable to poor hygiene while hypertension and diabetes can be traced to noise pollution through lack of sleep and rest. The health committee of the town union government took steps to assure that the team of Nigerian medical doctors based in the United States of America which come to Anambra state every summer to offer free medical services in selected communities included Ukpo community in the team's program in each of the three years of the town union government.

The health committee sought advice from the Dunukofia Local Government health division on what the town union could do to bring about improvement in the health conditions of the people in the community. The health committee found out that the local government will provide support for as many health posts as a community can establish the necessary infrastructure which is minimal, consisting of a one room building, a pit toilet and cans to carry water. The committee canvassed for provision of the minimal infrastructure among leaders of the four villages in the community. Within a short period of time each village established the necessary infrastructure for one health post making a total of four new health posts in addition to the already existing one. Impressed by this accomplishment, the health division of the local government rebuilt the broken health center building and established a second health center in the community[34]. The lesson of this experience is that through self-help efforts, a community can attract government investments in its development projects.

Chairman of the education committee hands out a scholarship check to a student while the president of the student wing (seated) and the president general (standing) of the Ukpo town union watch. Courtesy: Regency Photos.

The status of education in the Ukpo community presented as much challenges as health. In 2006, there were four public and two government accredited private primary schools and two public and one government accredited private secondary schools in the community. One of the public secondary schools, Ukpo Girls' Secondary School was for girls and the other, Ukpo Boys' Secondary School was for boys. All the primary schools, both public and private were fully enrolled in. There was hardly any child of primary school age that was not in school, a demonstration of the recognition of the importance of education by members of the community. The full enrollments were possible because Anambra state government provides primary education free in the public

---

[34] Hand Over Note from the Chairman UIU Health Committee: Hon.Elias Okafor. To the President General. 15th December 2008. Hon Elias A. Okafor.

schools. In addition, children of primary school age are available for school because they are not old enough to engage in income generating activities to help support their poor families.

But the story was different at the secondary school level. Enrollment was low in all the secondary schools, both public and private. Although the state government partially subsidizes secondary education in public schools many families cannot afford the costs of books, uniforms, etc. as well as numerous contributions of money which are frequently demanded of the students by the secondary school authorities. Additionally, many children drop out after primary school to engage in income generating activities in order to help support their poor families. This is more common among boys than girls. Boys engage as apprentices in small businesses where they hope to grow and begin to earn incomes as soon as possible.

The public schools were also poorly equipped in all respects including sports facilities, library books, laboratory equipment and even class room furniture. In all the schools, the buildings were in states of disrepair. Virtually all the school buildings were survivors of the Nigerian Civil (Biafra) War of 1967 to 1970 and were not renovated after the war. The public schools were poorly staffed especially in the areas of mathematics, sciences and English language and because of this the number of students who advance to universities was low. Most of the graduates of the secondary schools in the town did not qualify for admissions into universities. In summary, in 2006 the education system in Ukpo was in need of financial support for the students, adequate number of qualified teachers, provision of school materials and equipment and renovation of school buildings.

The education committee of the town union government that was headed by a Professor in a higher educational institution in the state faced the challenges in the education system in the town with considerable enthusiasm. The committee lobbied among the well-to-do members of the community for financial support for deserving students at the secondary and university levels. Within the first year of the town union in 2006 three individuals established separate scholarship programs for students at both secondary and university levels. One of the scholarship programs is a long term endowment based on a trust fund set up by the donor and managed by the chairman of the town union education committee. The youth wing of the Lagos branch of the town union government equipped a computer room with desktop computers and furniture and renovated one building in the Ukpo Boys' Secondary School. The state government through the effort of an Ukpo indigene in the government renovated one school building and provided water borehole in the Ukpo Girls' Secondary School.

One well-to-do member of the community constructed two lawn tennis courts in the premises of the Ukpo Boys' Secondary School. Two other well-to-do community members established a soccer team in the community and funded it. The team organizes annual competitions for secondary school students in the town. Because of the success of the soccer team the two sponsors were recognized by the town union government at the award ceremony during the Ukpo Day celebration of December 2007. That soccer team continued to grow in strength after the tenure of the town union government in 2008.In 2013 the team won the top position in a state-wide competition organized for the 177 communities in the state by the Anambra state government sports commission.

The education committee lobbied the state ministry of education and more teachers with better qualifications and experiences were posted to the public schools, both primary and secondary in the community. The committee also lobbied at the Anambra state office of the National Youth Service Corps which posted some Youth Service Corps members to teach in the secondary schools in the town. The town union government topped up the government stipend and provided housing for the Youth Service Corps members to make them happy. The education committee organized evening classes in mathematics and English language for the students and the town union government paid extra money to the teachers in those subjects to teach the evening classes.

The education system in Ukpo soon became the envy of parents in the neighboring communities who began to transfer their children from the secondary schools in their communities to those in Ukpo and enrollment rose dramatically in both of the public secondary schools in the town. The degree of envy which the successes in the efforts of the town union government education committee generated in neighboring communities can be illustrated with one true case story. A man from one of the neighboring communities went to the President General and asked that the numerous scholarships available to Ukpo students be extended to his children who had transferred to schools in Ukpo. The request could not be granted because of donor conditions all of which limited their programs to Ukpo indigenes[35].The man said that he regrets not being an indigene of Ukpo.

In 2007 the Anambra state Ministry of Education decided to merge secondary schools in several of the 177 communities and to make all schools co-educational in the state because of the low enrollments. But because of the increased enrollments in the two public secondary schools in Ukpo the ministry instead of merging them established a third one. The principals of the two original secondary schools wrote the town union government requesting that the new school be named and that the names of the pre-existing schools be changed because of the incongruity of boys graduating from a girls' secondary school and *vice versa*[36]. The town union government renamed the former Ukpo girls' Secondary School as Community Secondary School and the Ukpo Boys' Secondary School as Dunukofia High School and named the new secondary school as Walter Eze Memorial Secondary School in honor of the foremost patriot of the town. But a year later the state government Ministry of Education merged the Dunukofia High School and the Walter Eze Memorial Secondary School and the people of the town prefer the name Walter Eze Memorial Secondary School for the merged school.

To summarize, in 2006 orthodox health facilities in Ukpo were meagre and in poor states and the education system was in need of financial support for the students, adequate number of qualified teachers, provision of school materials and equipment and renovation of school buildings. The town union government through its committees on health and education was able to attract government investments that brought considerable improvements in both the health and education sectors in the community.

---

[35] Consideration for the 2007/2008 Award of the AdmoraOkunna Foundation Scholarships.To Stella C. Okunna. 14th January 2008.

[36] Request for Change of School Name. To President General, Ukpo Improvement Union, Ukpo. 17th Oct. 2006. Enemuo, I. I. and Okeke, P. C. Anambra State School System.

CHAPTER SIX

Security Measures

The contrast between Ukpo as a traditional and as a transitional society is palpable in the differences in the status of security of lives and property in the community. Security was an issue in Ukpo when the community was a traditional village. Robbery was the most common source of insecurity but people robbed mostly because they were hungry. Farm products mainly yam tubers and livestock such as goats and chicken were the most valuable assets that held attraction for thieves in the past. Money was valuable but there was not much of it and people typically buried the small amounts they had for safekeeping in the gardens. Women of means kept their valuables such as clothing and jewelry beyond the reach of thieves in the homes of prominent community members. Criminal members of Ukpo and neighboring communities scaled compound fence mostly in the dead of the nights[37]. If a man was starring he could intercept an intruder who at most carried a machete usually to be used only in self-defense.

If a thief was apprehended penalty was public humiliation. The thief would be paraded around the village with cursing and spitting at and with the item of attempted theft hung down his neck. Lynching was not part of the punishment for robbery only because murder on the soil of the Ukpo community was and still is a heinous offence against the gods of the people.

The punishments which were effective deterrents for crime were meted out in form of instant justice without trial of any form and the question of motive for the crime did not arise. For this reason, unfortunate people mostly defenseless women suffered punishments that were disproportionate to the crime of which they were accused. For example, a young widow was cast out of the family of her husband after her public parade for "stealing" a tuber of yam, probably driven by hunger, from her brother in-law barely a year after the death of her husband. She left behind her two boys; the younger one was a baby

---

[37] In the community people still live in walled compounds a heritage that was probably a security measure in the past.

under one year. The boys were later raised as orphans separately by different relatives[38].

British colonial administration sought to change the system dramatically by replacing the traditional system of justice with the British system. The colonial government established what they described as native court in Awka about 15 kilometers away from Ukpo and made instant justice without trial an offence punishable with a jail term. But the British justice system was also abused. The arrest process under the British system was as dehumanizing and painful as public parade of thieves under the traditional system. For example, the accused was first beaten into submission when necessary by the colonial police officer before he was handcuffed by tying both hands together with a rope. In that state he would be marched on foot for the distance of about 15 kilometers to the prison custody at Awka. If the police officer was senior enough to have an official bicycle the handcuffed accused was latched to the bicycle. As the officer rode the bicycle the accused trotted behind him at the speed of the bicycle generating a spectacle for people along the 15 kilometer road. Women suffered these and other sordid treatments because behind the colonial officers the women had no protection. The poor suffered more severe treatment than the wealthy from whom the police officer could expect some favor.

Justice was frequently manipulated at the trial stage. The colonial officers did not speak Igbo, the language of the people. Through the schools they established the colonial officers trained some people to serve as interpreters in the native court. Common cases of misinterpretations of statements in the court by the interpreters, sometimes out of ignorance and sometimes deliberately in return for backhander led to the frequent cases of the injustice of jailing the innocent under the colonial judicial system. One of the instances of deliberate misinterpretation must have served as an eye opener for the colonial judicial system in Awka. A primary school boy followed his father, an accused to the court. After the interpretation of the accused statement the judge was about to pronounce judgement against him when his son raised his hand. The judge recognized the boy and he told

---

[38] The widow was the author's grandmother and the older boy his father.

the court that the interpretation was different from what his father said. The interpreter did not object and the judge acquitted the boy's father[39].

Life under the shadow of imprisonment in the early days of the British colonialism gave rise to an expression, namely "until the white men depart nobody can deny the possibility of imprisonment" that is still in vogue in Ukpo as a metaphor used to describe inexorable circumstances. No matter how one lived the chance of imprisonment was real[40]. Sometime in Ukpo during the colonial period a pedestrian, the author's father was hit by a cyclist and he fell spilling his headload of farm produce. He paid money on demand to the cyclist "for repair of the vehicle" because of the fear of arrest and jail term for being knocked down by a cyclist[41].

Under the present state of transition to urban society, robbery remains the most common crime in Ukpo but the motive, sophistication and frequency are different. Presently people rob for the purpose of accumulating wealth. This motive is inspired by the process of urbanization which brought the well-to-do and the poor to live together in the same neighborhood. Before the transition poverty was not an issue since everybody was poor although some people produced more yams or kept a few more goats than others. But everybody lived in thatched huts, went about their businesses on foot, drew water from the same springs or puddles and medical care was provided for everybody by the same village medicine men. Inequality in income came with economic growth and dramatically changed the situation. The poor see the possibilities of wealth and seek the opportunity to acquire it including, for some people, criminal opportunities.

The robbers are now armed, some heavily and they kill anybody that may stand on their way. Ukpo indigenes among the criminals still respect murder on Ukpo soil as disgrace against the gods of the land. The criminals operate in gangs which include non-indigenes of Ukpo who pull the trigger when the need to kill arises. Changed population dynamics helps to elevate the frequency of armed robbery in the

---

[39] The school boy was the father of the present traditional leader of the Ukpo community and of the two great patriots of Ukpo, namely Walter and Arthur Eze.

[40] Obviously, at the time British occupation was considered a passing event.

[41] To own a bicycle at the time was to be elitist, a member of the upper-upper class who most probably worked in the white man's establishment as a domestic servant, a messenger, an interpreter, a nurse, or as a church and school teacher, etc.

community. The population is larger than in the past and it includes a large proportion of immigrants from outside the area as well as a large number of unemployed and under-employed people among who are secondary school leavers and university graduates.

Homes of the well-to-do members of the community are among the most common robbery targets by criminals looking to carry away expensive household electronic equipment such as television sets. Those homes are occupied during some weekends and holiday periods when the owners who usually reside outside the community are home for communal events which are more common during holiday seasons. The well-to-do hire paid guards to safeguard the property. But the guards are usually helpless under armed robbery attack and in some cases the guards are accomplices in the robberies. Business people who carry cash for transactions and wage workers especially on pay days are also common targets of robbery. Kidnaping for ransom emerged as a common form of crime in Eastern Nigeria when the banking system introduced innovations that render unnecessary carrying large amounts of cash for business transactions and when the values of household electronic equipment became less attractive to criminals robbing to get rich.

How did the town union face up to the challenge of elevated crime rate and sophistication in Ukpo following the process of transition to an urban society? The Ukpo vigilante is the state government recognized law enforcement unit of the town union. The unit has a wide range of responsibilities. Apart from crime control, the vigilante is also responsible for the enforcement of the various community laws, for maintenance of order during community gatherings such as community festivals and at individual events such as marriages and funerals that attract crowds in the community. The unit is supervised by the chairperson of the town union government security committee and it is headed by a commander that is appointed by the President General. The force is required to work closely with the Dunukofia Local Government division of the Nigerian federal government police force in Ukpo. Logistical support is minimal. The force is not to be armed because of a state law and during the tenure of the town union government from 2006 to 2008 motor vehicle available for the use of the unit was a personal motorcycle of the commander for which the town union paid the running expenses.

The vigilante is a volunteer force and except occasional gifts of money by some individuals in the community there was no financial remuneration for members mainly because of budget restrictions. The explanation that the President General used to appease representatives of the force when they complained was that the town union is a self-help organization and nobody is remunerated for the town union work. Instead of being paid some of the people who work for the town union contribute money voluntarily for the various causes of the community. The President General used his personal contribution to the town union which is substantial to support his point[42]. But to partially gratify the vigilante personnel the town union government approved that the unit should keep fifty percent of the amounts of monies they collect in fines from defaulters of the various community laws. This gesture served an additional purpose as motivation for the vigilante to be aggressive in enforcing the laws through collection of the fines.

ANEKWE'S COMPOUND,OBINAGU AKPU VILLAGE,UKPO

Serious gully erosions like this one claimed much land and threatened many homes in Ukpo community. Courtesy: Ukpo Improvement Union.

---

[42] Ukpo individual contributions, 2006 to 2008 and Jan to July 8, 2009.

But the vigilante had another challenge apart from poor logistics and no financial remuneration. Members were sometimes timid when they had to call to order the well-to-do and the powerful members of the community or friends and relations of such people. The President General intervened in many of such cases by personally leading the operations that involved such powerful people. The President General led in the initial effort to enforce the various environmental protection bylaws of which many of the well-to-do community members were defaulters.

Further interventions by the President General can be illustrated with specific examples. A well-to-do family in the community operated electronic public address system all night at the funeral of one of its members in defiance of the town union bylaw that banned the practice between the hours of 10.00 pm and 5.00 am. The family intimidated the vigilante force with the presence of a large number of the Nigerian police personnel that the family brought for the purpose from outside the Dunukofia Local Government Area. The President General went to the venue and advised the Nigerian police personnel to respect the community vigilante force by staying away from the matter. The President General took to the microphone and ordered the funeral proceedings to stop pending the payment of the required fine. The family grudgingly paid the fine before continuing the funeral proceedings.

In another case, a prominent member of the community who is a member of the cabinet of the traditional leader invited the Nigerian police of the Dunukofia Local Government Area division to arrest the commander of the vigilante for accosting his friend, a motorcycle taxi operator. The motorcycle operator carried a passenger in the night against the rule of the vigilante force which forbade motorcycle riders from carrying passengers at night. Criminals use motorcycles as getaway vehicles in snatching handbags from unsuspecting women. The President General was infuriated. He marched on foot with a great deal of indignation to the residence of the prominent community member and reminded him of the injustice of calling down rain on a child who is sent to deliver a head load of salt. The President General did not stop at that but went on to report the matter to the cabinet of the traditional leader. After the report the cabinet members were speechless, no member said a word; the action was embarrassing to the august body.

In spite of the numerous challenges, the vigilante proved to be effective to a good extent as deterrent for crime in Ukpo. Sure, there were some cases of robbery in the community during the tenure of the town union government from 2006 to 2008 but in most of such cases the culprits were apprehended and handed over to the Nigerian police for arrest as required. There were some cases of Ukpo indigenes accused of involvement in the rampant ransom kidnappings elsewhere in Anambra state outside the Ukpo community but the single incident of the crime in Ukpo which occurred in 2012, i.e. four years after the tenure of the town union government from 2006 to 2008 did not involve an Ukpo indigene as an accomplice. In comparison with most other communities the security situation in Ukpo was so calm during the tenure of the town union government of 2006 to 2008 that the management of the Rural Women Foundation, a United States based NGO that is working in Anambra state from Ukpo as its base hailed the town as safe and encouraging for their work. The organization came to Ukpo from a community in another state in Eastern Nigeria where the security situation was less conducive.

In summary, the process of transition from rural to urban society brought a different dimension of crime in the community. The law enforcement unit of the town union, namely the Ukpo vigilante was poorly motivated with no financial remuneration and with minimum logistics support. Yet the force was able to serve as deterrent to criminals and the community was comparatively peaceful during the tenure of the town union of 2006 to 2008. The encouragement in the forms of revenue sharing and leadership by example that the town union management provided to the members of the vigilante force contributed to the success of the law enforcement unit of the town union.

CHAPTER SEVEN

Collaboration with External Bodies and Role of Women in the Town Union Governance

The town union committee on collaboration with external bodies such as government agencies and an NGO during the period of 2006 to 2008 was chaired by a woman. There is needless confusion about the position of women in the town union government. The town union constitution of 1999 has provision for women's wing and does not exclude women from serving as members of the Central Executive but women did not serve until the 2006 to 2008 town union tenure.

Ukpo is a patriarchal society where women marry into the families of their husbands. This means that most married women in the community are from other communities. It is not considered prudent from security point of view for such women who are married from other communities to serve in the Central Executive particularly with frequent inter community feuds. Women of Ukpo origin married into families in the town were comparatively few. The probability of electing one of them into the town union Central Executive was low because there were only twelve constitutionally elected members of the Central Executive in three years. Because of this the women's wing is frequently erroneously viewed as a parallel town union government that is exclusive for the women. For example, the chairperson of the women's wing is unconstitutionally frequently addressed as President General of women Ukpo Improvement Union (the town union). This confusion helps to discourage election of women into the Central Executive of the town union.

In 2006 the town union government sought to correct this misconception by appointing two women as co-opted members to serve in the Central Executive. The 1999 constitution has provision which authorizes the town union government to co-opt people from the community to serve as members of the Central Executive along with elected members. Both women are of Ukpo origin and are married into families in the community. One of the two women was co-opted because she was involved in various activities and events in the community.

The second woman was appointed as a measure to help resolve a leadership problem in the women's wing of the town union at the time.

The women's wing was engulfed in a subversive row. The chairperson who completed her term would rather continue and because of that she colluded with some other members of the wing to make leadership difficult for her successor. The President General (2003 to 2005) had unsuccessfully tried with considerable amount of effort to resolve the dispute. The town union government of 2006 to 2008 drafted the new chairperson as the second woman in the Central Executive in order to enhance her authority and lessen the relative influence of the previous chairperson in the women's wing. That action worked. For the duration of the town union government from 2006 to 2008 the women's wing was at peace and it was clear that the wing is subordinate and not parallel to the Central Executive of the town union.

The first woman to be co-opted was assigned the role of chairperson of the committee that coordinated collaboration with external bodies which was a major committee of the town union government. In that role, the woman went beyond the terms of reference for her committee to become the *bona fide* woman leader in the town. She galvanized the women of the community to become active participants in various communal events. For example, she organized a large women dance troupe in which most married young women in the town participated. The group represented Anambra state at the national annual carnival in Abuja for three consecutive years. Through the effort of the same woman, two men's troupes also represented the state at the same events.

The chairperson of the town union committee on collaboration with external bodies, i.e. the *bona fide* women leader effectively represented the community interest at the state and local government levels. At the state and local governments she was appreciated because no other community had a woman playing that role. She brought back to Ukpo materials, information, and groups of people that were of specific relevance to women. For examples, she brought farm inputs including fertilizers and crop seeds; drugs for the local hospital to dispense; and equipment with which to establish small scale industries. These materials are provided by government for distribution in different communities but since the materials are not usually in sufficient amounts to go round only communities that are active in the government get them.

The *bona fide* women's leader attracted external bodies that provided essential services to the people of the community. For example, working with the town union health committee she made sure that the team of Nigerian medical doctors based in the United States of America which come to Anambra state every summer included Ukpo in their program in each of the three years of the town union government of 2006 to 2008. The team of doctors provides free medical services in selected communities. In 2006, an American based non-governmental organization (NGO), the Rural Women Foundation came to Ukpo through an indigene of the community who at the time was working at United States Agency for International Development in Abuja. The *bona fide* women's leader was at hand to provide guidance to the organization and contributed to the resounding impact that the NGO made in the community.

The NGO established office in Ukpo and since then has been providing services focused on vulnerable groups, essentially orphans and widows and widowers of HIV/AIDs victims, not only in Ukpo but also in several communities around the town. Some of the orphans and widows were themselves HIV positive. The NGO provided loans in cash and kind for the widows to engage in small scale businesses such as handcrafts and trading and supported the orphans in schools by providing them with school materials such as papers, pencils, and uniforms as well as teachers for extra classes in the evenings. The NGO put measures in place to ensure that the children's feeding improved by providing them with packages of protein enriched food for lunch at school; providing pulses for their mothers or stepmothers to cook at home; and educating the mothers to take advantage of vegetables that are widely available locally, some freely available in the gardens and in the wild. The NGO assisted members of the vulnerable groups with access to HIV retroviral drugs that were not available at the Nnamdi Azikiwe University Teaching Hospital in Ukpo, the largest hospital in the area.

The impact of the interventions by the NGO became palpable within a few months. The children who hitherto looked anemic and malnourished became robust with glossy skins. Their performance in school improved as they became more alert in their classes and their grades improved remarkably. In one occasion the children excelled in an Anambra state level quiz competition from which they emerged top first in the state.

Why was the Rural Women Foundation program for the orphans and vulnerable children so successful? The program was successful because it addressed a felt need; the interventions were properly targeted to the individuals who needed them; the individuals were well informed about what the program involved including what they would be provided for them; and the NGO had the privilege of local guidance. In addition their program was executed by locals who were familiar with the terrain.

The Rural Women Foundation has continued to work in the area from its office in Ukpo. A few years ago, the NGO proposed to establish a welfare center that will include an orphanage in Ukpo and secured a spacious property conveniently located adjacent to a secondary school and a primary school and less than one kilometer from the Nnamdi Azikiwe University Teaching Hospital. In 2016 the NGO began developing the property and is seeking funding for the center. A community member described the proposed program as a project of compassion because of the rampancy in the area of the type of problems the facility proposes to address. When in operation the center will be able to provide service for the entire Eastern Nigeria and beyond.

The NGO has built modern toilet facilities in two primary schools, in one of the two health centers in the community and at the Nnamdi Azikiwe University Teaching Hospital. Before then, the primary schools had pit toilets but the children, boys and girls, preferred open spaces within the school premises because the toilets were all the time in sordid conditions. At the Nnamdi Azikiwe University Teaching Hospital, there were no conveniences at all to serve out-patients, people who accompanied patients and other visitors to the hospital except the narrow open space within the hospital premises.

The *bona fide* women leader worked closely with a high ranking Ukpo woman in the Anambra state government and with the education committee of the town union to provide several infrastructural facilities for schools in the community. For example, within one year the state government renovated the administrative building and provided a water borehole at the Girls' Secondary School in the Ukpo community. At that time, public schools in the state were unequipped and their infrastructural facilities were in states of disrepair.

In Nigeria, national population census is conducted once in ten years and voter registration once in four years. This means that not all town union governments are burdened with the task of executing those activities in the community since a town union government each has a tenure of only three years. But by coincidence the town union government of 2006 to 2008 executed the two activities, national population census in 2006 and voter registration in 2007. Both are politically charged activities in Nigeria because political rights and privileges are based on them. For example, representations in first three tiers of governments; distribution of federal resources; and creation of new states, local governments, and other political constituencies are based on population size. Similarly, large numbers of registered voters are important especially to politicians because majority vote is a determinant of winners in all popular elections in the country.

In Nigeria, population censuses are conducted by the National Population Commission. The commission had a local government office in Ukpo which was headed by a local government census officer that was a woman at the time. The National Population Commission sent a team of enumerators from outside the community to conduct the census under the supervision of the local government census officer. After the enumeration, the commission sent a team of law enforcement officers from outside the state to verify the count.

Although it had no official government role in the conduct of the census, the town union government nevertheless engaged in an extensive awareness campaign to make sure that community members understood the significance of the census and the imperative that every resident of the community stood up to be counted. The town union government constituted a committee to supervise the conduct of the census on behalf of the community. The committee was headed by an experienced Professor in a higher educational institution who was assisted by the woman chairperson of the town union government committee that coordinated collaboration with external bodies. The town union government committee on the census employed a large number of community members and organized classes for them on how to mobilize members of the community to stay home for the census and on how to complete the census enumeration forms.

When the government team of enumerators arrived in the town to conduct the census the town union government made them comfortable by providing them free housing, food and transportation irrespective of what their employer, the National Population Commission had provided for them. The town union also provided logistical support in terms of transportation for the census officer for her supervisory work in Ukpo and protected her from pressure mounted on her by community members for employment to work as government census enumerators in other communities in the Dunukofia Local Government Area. Some of the cases of the pressure were unkind. For example, a local politician asked that his wife be employed. When he did not succeed he plotted to have the census officer transferred out of the Dunukofia Local

77

Government Area on made up excuses. The town union government called him to order reminding him that his case amounted to vendetta because he had asked for a favor that was not granted.

The town union census workers went to each household on the eve of each household's enumeration to ensure that all members would be home the following day for the counting. The town union census workers took the federal government enumerators to each household and in many cases took over the enumeration; the government enumerators cared less. At the end of each day, the town union government workers sat down together with the government enumerators and in some cases without them and reviewed completed enumeration forms for accuracy.

About two weeks after the enumeration two young army officers came from the National Population Commission to verify the conduct of the census. They too worked like the federal government enumerators with limited interest in their work. The attitude of both teams from the National Population Commission to their work was convenient for the town union government because the census was conducted to the satisfaction of the town union. Unfortunately, the published result of the census was bulked at the local government level and population of the town was not published.

The voter registration was conducted in 2007 by the Independent National Election Commission which also had a local government office in Ukpo. The office was also headed by a woman. This activity was as important to the community as the census conducted the previous year but it was of particular interest to local politicians. The local politicians voluntarily covered the financial costs to the town but depended on the town union government experience of the 2006 census for logistics. The conduct of the voter registration followed the same pattern as the conduct of the census. The federal government staff attitude to their work and the town union government role were both similar to the 2006 census. The town union government used the same census committee for the conduct of the voter registration. The committee also deployed the same work force it used for the census. The voter registration result was revealing. It showed that there were more than 22,000 qualified voters, i.e. the population of people of 18 years and above in the town.

To summarize, the town union organization in Ukpo for the first time in its history beginning in 1944 included women as members of its Central Executive. One of the women was elected chairperson of the town union government committee on collaboration with external bodies. The committee brought to the community investments in health, education and agriculture by government and a non-governmental organization and played effective roles in the conducts of the national population census and voter registration in the community. Under the leadership of the woman chairperson the town union government assured that both federal government activities were conducted with reasonable levels of accuracy.

CHAPTER EIGHT

Faith as a Resource and as a Challenge

From 2006 to 2008 faith served as a valuable resource as well as a source of a resolute challenge for the town union governance. For example, heathen faith was a valuable asset in the non-violent resolution of the intercommunity conflicts and in maintenance of law and order in the Ukpo community during the period. For their position on non-violent resolution of the conflicts with neighboring communities, the leaders of Ukpo community found a formidable ally in the faith of the Ukpo people in a non-violence god in the community. Agitators for violent approach to the resolution of the conflicts were quick to reconsider their stand when they were reminded of the dire consequences of bloodshed by an Ukpo indigene on Ukpo soil.

The non-violence god is a spirit; it has a name, *Ajana*, but unlike other heathen deities in the community it has no physical image to represent it. It resides in certain bushes that are protected for it in different corners around the town. The spirit is a sin eater god; with appropriate petition rituals it sucks up the transgressions of people and keeps the society clean of evils. People petition it for forgiveness of wrong-doings and its forest abodes serve as disposal grounds for mysterious objects of unknown origin such as may be placed with diabolic intentions by enemies against individuals or against the community. To this deity bloodshed within the Ukpo territory by an Ukpo indigene is a "no-no" with steep appeasement penalties for default irrespective of whether the blood is that of an Ukpo person or that of another person from anywhere. The motive is irrelevant; penalty applies even in cases of accidental murder such as can occur in hunting expeditions.

The faith in the deity continues to serve as a deterrent to violent crimes in the community. The value to an Ukpo criminal of any amount of stolen items cannot compensate for the steep penalties for a crime which results in death in the town. Part of the deity's penalty for murder is banishment from the community that, in some cases would be for life but cannot be less than a year; the duration is determined by soothsayers[43]. The penalties are stretched to members of the extended family of the perpetrator. For example, if the culprit refuses to leave town in banishment the non-violence god will haunt members of his extended family with different forms of adversity such as sickness, death, or economic distress. The banishment penalty created enclaves of settlements of people of Ukpo origin in several communities in Eastern Nigeria as some of the people who were banished for life survived and raised families in their host communities.

One of the forest abodes of the non-violent spirit deities in the Ukpo community. Courtesy: Regency Photos.

Marriage of a wife for the victim's family in compensation for the death of its member is another part of the penalty for murder in addition to banishment. Successful implementation of the marriage reparation depends on the co-operation of the victim's family. There are cases of victim's families refusing to accept a wife either because no member wants such a wife or because of vendetta. The perpetrator's extended family suffers the curse of the non-violence god until that part of the

---

[43] The banishment, in addition to appeasement of the non-violence god, also helps to protect the perpetrator from retributive justice from angry relations of the victim.

penalty is fulfilled. In the town, some families are still atoning for murders that resulted from slavery of long ago.

Faith in this deity is still compelling in Ukpo today. For example, in 2010 a young man, who was a member of a prominent family in the community, while driving a car got involved in an accident in which a motorcycle rider died in the town. The young man left the town for a period of one year and his family paid the costs for the marriage of a wife to the family of the motorcycle rider. It did not matter that the motorcycle rider was on the wrong side of the road or that he carried marijuana in his pocket at the time of the accident.

Considerable tensions were generated in the community at the intersection of faith and culture. The tensions posed the greatest of all the internal challenges that the town union faced during the period 2006 to 2008. The tensions were generated by Christian opposition to the efforts to revive the Opotor festival of music and dance during the tenure of the town union and in the enforcement of Ukpo constitutional provisions on cultural days by the town union government. In anticipation of this problem, the President General in his acceptance speech at his inauguration on December 29, 2005 made the point that under his leadership in the community individual faiths must be respected (Appendix I). Emphasis was on a philosophy, namely "onyenachieonyenachie" i.e. mind your god or God and leave others with theirs that was attributed to one Sarah[44]. Expression of an impression that one god or God is superior to another including an attempt at forced conversion is comparable to an insult on one's mother which in the community is resisted with as much force as one can muster.

Yet, Christian opposition proved to be a serious source of declining interest in the celebration of the Opotor festival which some Christians consider a heathen festival. The festival is a major cultural event with high social values in the community. Some light minded Christians associate costumes with heathenism. But the more objective basis for the Christian opposition is that the festival has a matriarch idol. Some

---

[44] The author's maternal grandmother reported that sometime in the past one Sarah would walk about in the market square all day every Oye market day chanting "onyenachieonyenachie". Sarah was half human and half god; she was addressing nobody in particular but people took note because her statement made sense.

Opotor celebrants voluntarily pay homage at the shrine of the idol during the festival days.

A memo approved by the town union government and signed by the President General in January 2006 requesting the Christian churches in the community to delay their Sunday morning masses to 9.00 o'clock in the morning of the day of grand finale of the Opotor festival in February infuriated some church leaders[45]. The aim of the request was to allow night masquerades that are not to be seen to clear the streets. A few years before, early church goers, a man and his wife confronted the night masquerades while driving to church. The collusion resulted in physical injury and dent to their car. The couple was blamed because they should have known better than to be in the street at such an unholy hour on the sacred day. But written withdrawal of the memo did not assuage one parish priest[46]. The priest waylaid a masked dancer and beat him up in his costume. He ordered his parishioners not to participate in the grand finale of the festival.

But that grand finale was rated by the people as one of the most successful in the recent history of the festival. The grand finale was widely attended in terms of both performers and spectators by members of Ukpo and neighboring communities including members of the particular priest's church. As if in purposeful defiance of the priest's order, two leading members of the church approached the President General at the grand finale venue and congratulated him for what they described as a wonderful performance. The following Sunday, the priest lamented in his sermon that there were no Christians in his congregation. He was right if he defined a Christian as someone who did not perform heathen rites because in Ukpo, virtually everybody performs heathen rites, though Christians perform them covertly.

The 1999 constitution of the Ukpo community set aside five days during December holiday season each year for communal events forbidding all private events. The days are Saturday before Christmas, Ofala Day; December 26, Ukpo Day; December 29, second town union Convention Day; December 30, Village Meeting Day; and December 31,

---

[45] The 2007 Opotor Festival in Ukpo addressed to the Parish Priest, St Simons Catholic Church, Ukpo on January 30, 2007 by Felix Nweke and Emma Nwankwo.

[46] Re-Your Letter to Parish Priest, St Simon's Parish, Ukpo with Regards to "the 2007 Opotor Festival in Ukpo addressed to the President General/Secretary General, Ukpo Improvement Union, Ukpo by Ilokolobia, Ignatious E.

Age Grade Meeting Day. These dates are at conflict with annual three day crusades by several Christian groups who aim at dates when many citizens of the community will return home. Because of this, every December holiday season, the town union organization and the cabinet of the traditional leader jointly circulate a memo and follow it up with a public announcement by a town crier reminding the community about the constitutional provision[47]. An attempt by one Pentecostal church group to defy the constitution and stage a crusade during December 29 to 31, 2006 was stopped in the process by the community vigilante force.

In 2007, Catholic Churches in Ukpo advertised through posters a three day holiday season crusade during December 29 to 31 in defiance of the constitutional provision[48]. Several groups and individuals including leading members of the churches tried but failed to discourage this development which amounted to confrontation. The churches claimed the right of freedom of worship as provided by the Nigerian constitution. The argument was that the churches could express freedom of worship in their premises even if it is against the constitution of the community which accommodates the premises. As in the case of the Pentecostal church a year earlier, the crusade was stopped in the process by the community vigilante force.

The leaders of the affected churches were enraged. The same priest who interfered with the Opotor festival a year earlier claimed that the President General assaulted him physically. In a peace meeting called by the cabinet of the traditional leader the parish priest came with a large crowd of members of his congregation and was adamant in demanding that the President General must resign and at the same time apologize to the churches for peace to prevail in Ukpo. The priest seemed to have a convoluted perception of his influence in the community based on the size of his constituency, namely his congregation which is large and because on matters of faith Christians are not expected to hold independent views but to follow the views of their leaders without reasoning. But those stipulations did not work in the priest's favor.

For the continuation of the peace meeting a week later the priest arrived with just two persons and was mellow, no more demand for the

---

[47] Regulated End of Year Activities: A Reminder. Max. Nwobor.

[48] Crusade! Crusade!! Crusade!!! by Innocent Agunwa and Josephat Okafor

resignation of the President General or for his apology to the churches. What happened since the first peace meeting? A group of women went to the priest to express embarrassment for the supposed action of the town union government. The priest told them to state their embarrassment in writing and collect signatures. But the women failed to collect a reasonable number of signatures. One leading member of the church went to the meeting of the Age Grade to which he and the President General belonged and moved a motion that the President General be dismissed from the Age Grade, he was booed. The parish priest reported the case to the state police but hastily withdrew the report, most likely on the order of his Bishop. The priest was later sent away in what can pass as a punitive transfer from a large church in Ukpo, a semi-urban town to a small church in a remote village community.

Trailing the churches' outrage and incitement, the weeks that followed were tense in the community. All over the town, people gathered in informal small groups and engaged in discussions of the matter, in some cases with considerable tension. What transpired in one informal group discussion is illuminating. A group of five women stood at a point along a farm road discussing the event with much tension, some in support of the church and some in support of the town union government. A sixth woman with a hoe and a machete who was on her way to the farm stopped for the discussion and right away engaged in a verbal attack on the President General referring to him as a heathen. One of the original five women reminded her where two of them met the previous night. The farm implements fail off the hands of the sixth woman and she ran down the farm road only to run back up as involuntarily as she ran down. She pleaded with the five original women not to mention the incident anywhere else. What happened was that the night before as one of the five original women was waiting her turn in the shrine of a soothsayer in the community the sixth woman came out of a dark room with the soothsayer behind her.

At the bottom of the hostility by the leaders of various churches in the community towards the town union government was that in 2006 the President General in his private capacity organized Ukpo people who did not confess Christianity to form a group. The aim was that with group identity they would be able to confess their non-Christian religious convictions without the fear of being called names. This arrangement worked very well. The group meets regularly and performs their religious rites for themselves openly and for Christians privately. Funerals of their members are announced community wide by a town crier and the members gather in large numbers to perform the funeral rites. People are able to declare with pride that they are heathens or that they are not Christians.

Many men and married women of various ages joined the group and membership grew at a geometric rate. The only groups of people in the community who did not join were single women who feared that being called heathen would discourage potential husbands. Those of them who cared less about husbands were barred by their parents. But the young women continued to practice their heathen faith in private. Clarissa Pinkola Estes is right; women's life is like dessert plants that are scanty on the surface but lush underground[49].

In summary, in some respects faith served as a resource and in other respects as a source of tension that posed serious challenges to community governance. Faith served as a valuable resource to the town union especially in the effort to resolve intercommunity conflicts without violence. Faith also served as a deterrent to violent crime in the community. Faith as a resource derived from the strong beliefs by members of the Ukpo community in the potency of a non-violence spirit god which imposes steep penalties for bloodshed by an Ukpo indigene within the territory of the community.

But faith was also a source of serious challenge to the town union government during the period of 2006 to 2008. The confluence of culture and faith generated dangerous conflicts between the town union and some Christian leaders. The Christian leaders were hostile to the town union and opposed its measures principally because of the action of the President General in organizing, in his personal capacity non-Christian members of the community for the purpose of protecting their faith through group identity. The organization of non-Christians also helped to promote cultural activities which the town union government would not promote because of determined Christian opposition.

[49] Estes, Clarissa Pinkola. 1995. Women who run with the wolves: Myths and stories of the wild woman archetype. Ballantine Books. New York.

CHAPTER NINE

Leadership Style

At the maiden meeting of the incoming town union government in January 2006, distribution of responsibilities among members of the Central Executive was the principal item in the agenda. Earlier, on 29 December 2005, at the inauguration of the incoming town union government, the incoming President General had enumerated priority activities and projects in the areas of conflict resolution, environmental protection, sanitation, cultural revival, health, education and security needs (Appendix I). The priority activities and projects were compiled in advance by the elected members of the new town union government in a pre-inauguration meeting during which the inauguration address of the President General was reviewed.

Committees were constituted to provide leadership in each of the priority areas except conflict resolution that was considered a sensitive matter and which was being supervised by the Ukpo Security Council. A democratic process was followed in choosing members of the committees. Nominations were extended to all Ukpo people within and outside the town union government membership. The aim was to bring in capable people to join in the execution of the town union government agenda. Non-members of the Central Executive who were elected to serve in a committee were co-opted to join the Central Executive as full members. Officers of a committee, including the Chairman were elected by members of the committee. Each committee was allowed full responsibility and free hand to execute the functions assigned to it and report to the Central Executive of the town union government in the scheduled monthly meetings of the town union. The scheduled monthly meetings became discussions of committee reports in nature.

Town union governments present reports to the Ukpo community twice in a year in the community gatherings called UIU (Ukpo Improvement Union) Convention. Each year, the first convention is the last Oye market day in September, i.e. Yam Festival weekend and the second one is on December 29. The town union government (2006 to 2008) presentations at these conventions were also in the form of committee reports that were rendered by the chairpersons of the committees who were often applauded at the gatherings. With the understanding that a progressive leader is one who is more interested in making group members feel like leaders than in him/her being seen as the leader, the President General was present in each occasion, whether in monthly meetings of the Central Executive or at UIU conventions, acknowledging along with the rest of the people each committee's achievements as their chairpersons showed off leadership in their assigned responsibilities.

The President General makes acceptance speech at his inaugural on December 29, 2005. Courtesy: Regency Photos.

The scheduled monthly and emergency meetings of the Central Executive frequently sat for long hours often from 10.00 am to 7.00 pm. Lunch was provided at each meeting. When budget was tight as was often the case the President General asked for donation from among the members at the meeting. The President General did not eat until everybody had gotten food.

Occasionally members of the community gave presents to the members of the Central Executive; cows were commonly given at Christmas and New Year. Sharing of such gifts was in form of exciting festivals. The animals were slaughtered at the residence of the President General and shared equally spread out on a mat of banana leaves in full view of all members. In all cases the President General was the last to take a share. At the first occasion that the gifts were shared, i.e. in December 2006, a certain elected member with a high office in the Central Executive opposed the equal sharing arguing that co-opted members would not take as much share as elected members. He was supported by some other elected members. The President General expressed outrage at the suggestion and made it known to everybody that he considered all members equal and that being elected rather than co-opted member did not make a difference as long as everybody performed his or her assigned responsibilities.

One of the first tasks of the town union government was to define citizenship of the Ukpo community. Ukpo is a patriarchal society but also recognizes three kinship relationships: father's family, mother's family, and family of in-laws (ikwuato, namely: ikwunna or umunna, ikwunne and ikwuogo or ndiogo). The word bastard has no meaning in Ukpo. Two options await children born outside wedlock: those whose mothers never marry belong fully to the families of their mothers. Others, whenever their mothers marry, are adopted by their mothers' husbands as part of the marriages. Abandoned children belong to the families of whoever picked them up. Official adoption has become popular in Eastern Nigeria and it is embraced by Ukpo people. Against this backdrop, town union government defined full citizenship as being born to an Ukpo father or mother; being married to an Ukpo man; or being adopted by an Ukpo citizen. In Nigeria residency, no matter the duration does not confer to people resident status in a town. One is always considered to come from where the father comes from.

The town union government also decided that a former President General should continue to be addressed as President General. The aim of this gesture is to encourage such people who had acquired sufficient experience through service to continue to provide leadership in the community. In Ukpo, a President General is the leader of the entire community, second only to the traditional leader.

The Ukpo community was mobilized for support of the agenda of the present town union government by a number of rousing factors. The tenure of the town union government was variously described by some as tumultuous and by others as eventful. The tenure was dense with activities and events some of which were controversial and inspired extensive informal public debates. For examples, the hostility of various church groups towards the town union government led to informal group discussions garnering at the same time sympathy and incomprehension for the town union government. The two land litigations with neighboring communities picked up momentum and added impetus to the excitement. As the people waited from one court sitting to another they anticipated the outcome with considerable anxiety. The sanitation committee members and vigilante personnel were visibly all over the place. Sanitation committee members were cleaning public spaces and the vigilante personnel were collecting fines from defaulters. The presence of the town union government everywhere and all the time created a significant amount of excitement that no one could miss.

The town union government of 2000 to 2002 recognized, in an award ceremony eight members of the Ukpo community who attained the highest positions in their places of work and businessmen that were considered successful in honest businesses. The current town union government viewed that as an eloquent gesture with potential to motivate the people of the community to aspire to excel in their various endeavors. The current town union government implemented an expanded version of it by making the award ceremony an annual event and by extending recognition to grassroots community members and to non-Ukpo indigenes that were posted by government and other agencies to serve in the community.

For example, in 2006, the medical director in charge of Nnamdi Azikiwe University Teaching Hospital Ukpo campus who is not an Ukpo indigene was one of those recognized on Ukpo Day that year. A young woman of Ukpo origin who was recognized at Harvard University in the United States for academic excellence was among the people that were recognized on the Ukpo Day of 2007. On Ukpo Day of 2008 at the end of the tenure of the town union government, fifteen people were recognized for their courage in defense of the Ukpo constitution.

Fairness in handling the affairs of the community earned the respect of the community for the leadership as courageous. Impartiality and courage in the leadership of the town union were on display in enforcing constitutional provisions and bylaws of the community in which powerful people and relations of the President General were treated equally with the less powerful and with non-relations. There were some powerful people who acted as if the laws are not made for them and the matter of relationships is an important factor in enforcing laws in a rural and traditional setting such as the Ukpo community. People were on the look out to see how the leader would handle situations when his relations and when powerful people were affected (Appendix III).

A wealthy and the most powerful member of the community, Arthur Eze owned an apartment building in the community. Occupants of the property defaulted on the bylaw against the channeling of domestic liquid waste into the streets[50]. Enforcement campaign started from there. Arthur who was sympathetic with the sanitation course gracefully paid the fine on behalf of his tenants and joined the campaign team. The next ports of call were the homes of the traditional leader of the community, that of his deputy, and those of the relations of the President General of the community in that order. Thereafter, many people hastily cleaned up the surroundings of their residences and business premises to beat the arrival of the enforcement campaign team.

One event involving the same powerful man was more dramatic. He planned a funeral wake in which who was who in Nigeria as a whole would attend. The town union government Central Executive held an emergency meeting on the funeral and discussed among other things waiver of the bylaw against operation of public address system beyond 10.00 o'clock in the night of the wake keep. The President General proposed waiver arguing that enforcement would be difficult considering the number and status of the people who would participate. The President General also argued that the celebrant merited special consideration because of his high sense of patriotism and philanthropy in the community. The President General's proposal was defeated in a popular vote by a wide margin. The celebrant acknowledged that he was aware of the law when the President General reminded him about it prior to the event.

The crowd was overwhelming, security forces both police and army was everywhere. As time approached 10.00 o'clock in the night the

---

[50] To refer to Arthur Eze as the wealthiest man in the context of Ukpo community will be a gross understatement of his wealth because he is one of a handful of Nigerian members of Fortune 500.

President General pushed his way through the crowd and through the security forces to draw the celebrant's attention to time. The man flared up. That the security forces did not arrest or even rough handle the President General surprised everyone. Perhaps the members of the security forces were confused by the courage of the President General.

The President General left town that night and submitted his resignation letter from his hiding the following day[51]. On the second day the traditional leader discovered his whereabouts and pleaded that he returned to help receive a former head of state of the country that was paying a condolence visit. At that occasion the President General was honored with the assignment of reading a welcome address that allowed him to shake hand with the ex-head of state. At the end of that event, Arthur Eze invited the President General and his close aides to his home, congratulated the President General for his courage, and gave him 1,000,000 Naira for town union government work and 500,000 Naira to share with the close aides who accompanied him. To the dissatisfaction of the close aides the President General ruled that the whole money be paid into the town union account for town union government work. When these things were reported at the meeting of the Central Executive, members took sides with the aides but the President General stood his ground arguing that the town union needed money.

But the first display of courage by the town union government was in its first year on December 16, 2006. On December 2, 2006, without reference to the town union government the cabinet of the traditional leader passed a law to reintroduce a ban on all private celebrations from December 15 to January 1 each holiday season that was lifted under the previous town union government. When the President General learnt about it, he took steps and stopped public announcement of it and later on December 16, he addressed a joint session of the cabinet and the Central Executive on the subject titled "Mutual Respect among Leadership Institutions at Ukpo" (Appendix II).

In strong words, the President General warned, in effect that he would not condone a parallel executive government. He warned that the cabinet should stay away from executive functions of the town union

---

[51]Position of President General, Ukpo Improvement Union.To Raphael Akude. June 26, 2008. Felix Nweke.
  Position of President General, Ukpo Improvement Union.To Felix Nweke. 28th June 2008. Raphael Akude.

government and concentrate on its traditional role. It was a frontal attack on the cabinet whose authority had not been challenged before. Its senior members were enraged by the address, most of them turned red in the face, one got up perhaps to speak but sat back down without speaking. The traditional leader saved the day. He ruled that the President General's objection was sustained and the matter was rested. The cabinet had sometimes usurped the power of the town union government because successive town union governments subjugated themselves to the cabinet by default. The cabinet had often executed essential functions that successive town union governments neglected.

Accountability, especially in handling money was a valuable leadership asset. Although transparent expenditure accounts are not possible under Nigerian circumstances, income account through periodic display of list of voluntary contributions enabled community members to know how much money was coming in[52]. They could then get some idea of how much was going out by observing what the town union government was doing in the community and with regards to the land litigations. The generous donation by the President General which the people knew about through the income account became evident that he was leading by example.

In the Nigerian context, anybody who is in a position of authority of any sort would be tempted with money by people seeking favor. With regard to apresident general of the Ukpo town union such temptation is most common by politicians who sought help in mobilizing members of the community for vote. The President General did not side with any political party. Constitutionally a president general of the Ukpo town union should not be a member of a political party so that he can neutrally receive any politician on behalf of the community. Participation in partisan politics by president generals will egg on the politicization of the town union and undermine its integrity as a community based self-help organization.

Other people who would like a president general to support their cases in disputes also commonly tempt him with money and other gifts. It did not take long before it became clear to all that the President General 2006 to 2008 did not accept gifts including money. It was also understood that he did not act on the basis of gossip. Reports which

---

[52] Ukpo individual contributions, 2006 to 2008 and January to July 8, 2009.

were brought to him in private which he required in writing were discussed in the presence of all concerned. This had the effect of significantly cutting down the number of such reports.

In conclusion, progressive leadership style is central to the success of the town union in achieving its stated goals. Courage, fairness, selflessness, and compassion are virtues of leadership that worked in favor of the town union government. Courage was required to pursue evenhandedness; without selflessness courage would lead to dictatorial governance that would be short in compassion.

Leadership style impacts on the leader as it impacts on the people. For example, when a leader lifts the people up by addressing their felt needs the people stand on his shoulders and hail him, he becomes taller by their height that is added to his. On the other hand if the leader steps down on the people, by embezzling their money for example, the people's struggle to free them from his hold pulls him down and he becomes a lesser person. Long after he left office the President General (2006 to 2008) continues to be a revered member of the Ukpo community. His appearance in gatherings is often received with applause. In contrast, the President General (2012 to 2014) is rarely seen in the town after he left office in 2014. Yoruba people of the South-West Nigeria call attention to the fate of retrogressive leadership in their communities through a metaphor, namely "Nineteen that will not associate with One has no chance of being Twenty".

CHAPTER TEN

Sustainability Concerns

As the tenure of the town union government progressed some members of the community began to express concerns that the town union administration was setting a standard that would be difficult to sustain and the levels of courage and fairness hard to replicate. The town union institution does not have a bureaucracy and although members can serve three consecutive terms if re-elected the institutional memory which that arrangement can provide hardly helps. The President General can serve only one three year term in twelve years and each one comes with his own agenda that are dependent on the individual's personal goal, perspective, and worldview.

Following these concerns, the Constitution Review Committee on the Rotation of the Offices of the town union institution was set up in a joint meeting of the cabinet of the traditional leader and the town union government held on March 24, 2008 to review the system of rotation of offices. The committee observed that the territorial integrity of Ukpo was under a serious attack from hostile neighbors and the security situation in Ukpo more precarious than in 1999 when the constitution for the governance of the community was fashioned[53]. The committee noted that everything humanly possible should be done to sustain the current internal peace existing in Ukpo so that the community would remain united in the legal war with external aggressors. The committee further observed that the town was in a special situation and needed a special person as President General. The land cases in courts were at their critical stages and the town could not afford to lose either of the cases. The committee also noted that the President General the town needed at the time should be a special person with the following qualities: impeccable patriotism, immense political will, unwavering commitment to the cause of Ukpo, very high integrity, selfless, trustworthy, foresighted, focused, and a high ability to mobilize funds.

The committee recommended that the four villages in the town among which the offices of the town union government rotated be

---

[53] Report.Constitution Review Committee on the Rotation of Offices of Ukpo Improvement Union (UIU).

grouped into two by merging Oranto, the largest in terms of population with Akaezi, the smallest and merging the two middle ones, Isiekwulu and Akpu and that the offices of the town union government be rotated between the two groups of villages. The aim was that the first group, namely Oranto and Akaezi to which the incumbent President General belonged and which would start the new rotation cycle, if approved, would reelect the same President General for another three year term. The incumbent President General did not participate in any of these. He was not at the joint meeting of the cabinet and the town union government of March 24, 2008 at which the Constitution Review Committee was set up. He was not even aware of the establishment of that committee until its report was presented.

The committee recommendation was accepted but not implemented. Before the tenure of the incumbent President General people were pleaded with to take the position. The position was not attractive because it had no financial inducement. But the position had acquired high status under the same President General and made the incumbent more respectable in the community. The result is that even in the absence of financial remuneration people now lobby and campaign for the position.

The President General himself was also troubled by genuine concern for sustainability of the town union government's measures and achievements and was thinking of a suitable successor. An individual that came to mind from the next village that would produce his successor under the existing arrangement had the necessary courage and stature for the job but he was short in selflessness. But if the right successor could not be identified for the next town union government, what of the government after that; would there be a suitable person after the following three years? The President General targeted a member representing Isiekwulu village in his town union government. Isiekwulu village will produce the President General after the following three years. This member followed the President General to the frontline of all the town union government efforts even in the cases of immense tension as were frequent when enforcing laws against powerful members of the community.

On December 29, 2008 a new President General was inaugurated for the three year period 2009 to 2011 and the one before him became President General (2006 to 2008). The President General (2006 to 2008) stayed in the community for another three years up to the year 2011 and continued to pursue the land litigations as a private citizen. He left after the court cases were both ruled in favor of Ukpo. On December 20, 2011 in his unpublished valedictory address titled "Thank You" at the 2011 Ofala festival the outgoing President General of 2009 to 2011 appreciated the extra efforts of the President General (2006 to 2008) by saying "…the immediate past President General … You have shown us what is expected of a patriot. You have volunteered your time and resources to the continued service of your people beyond your tenure and we owe a major part of our successes to your will"[54].

The process of electing the President General for the period 2012 to 2014 by the Isiekwulu village was loaded with accusations of manipulations of the election process. The member of the 2006 to 2008 town union government from this village who was being targeted for the position this time by the President General (2006 to 2008) was the obvious choice in the minds of most people. The targeted member played along by expressing willingness to serve. But as the campaign heated up he backed down citing lack of family support as his reason. It turned out that he could not take the pressure of the position; he was more effective as a follower than as a leader.

The candidate which the village nominated for the position was turned down at the joint cabinet of the traditional leader and town union government meeting that endorses candidates as required by the constitution. The village was having difficulties in providing another candidate. The cabinet of the traditional leader unilaterally without the town union government (2009 to 2011) mandated its members from the village to provide a candidate who was inaugurated at the Opotor festival of February 2013. Objections raised by both the village concerned and the President General (2006 to 2008) against this unconstitutional action were ignored[55]. That President General (2012 to 2014) was later found guilty of embezzlement of the town union moneys[56]. He was suspended from the cabinet of the traditional leader of which he was a member and he was not allowed to perform the President General's end of term duties in December 2014 when his tenure ended.

---

[54] Thank You. 24th December 2011. Ofodile Okafor.

[55] Prof Felix Nweke. Appointment of President General of Ukpo Improvement Union (UIU).To Igwe in-Council, Care of the Cabinet Secretary, Ukpo, Dunukofia. Copy: Secretary General, Ukpo Improvement Union (UIU). October 22, 2013.

[56] Ukpo Improvement Union (UIU) Audit Report Part 2 Content-Audited Report, Observations and Recommendation (March 2013 to May 2014).

From 2011 the sustainability concerns began to show worrying evidence of being confirmed. Security of lives and property which before then was scarcely an issue deteriorated. In that period Eastern Nigeria was under the grip of ransom kidnapping. On July 29, 2012 the traditional leader of Ukpo community was himself abducted. The toilet facility that the NGO, the Rural Women Foundation provided in a primary school was vandalized. Town criers returned to using mobile electronic equipment through the town from mid-nights to early mornings. The five days set aside in the constitution during the December holiday season each year for communal events became abused. Various church groups resumed their three day crusades within those five days and operated electronic public address systems all night in each occasion unchecked. On December 31, 2013 an eminent member of the community celebrated the highest title in the town and invited not only members of the Ukpo community but also all titled men and women in the entire Dunukofia Local Government Area. The traditional leader, the President General (2006 to 2008), and the President General (2012-2014), i.e. the incumbent, participated.

But the abuse of December 26 should be of greatest concern to members of Ukpo community because the setting aside of that day as Ukpo Day evokes an emotional history. The Ukpo Day was established by Dr. Walter Eze in the early 1980s because he was saddened by the fact that members of the Ukpo community trooped in their masses to the neighboring town of Abagana to celebrate the holiday season. The Abagana community celebrates their equivalent of Opotor festival at the end of the year between Christmas and New Year. On December 26, 2013 a leading member of the Ukpo community invited all the women in Ukpo to his home to celebrate the season with distribution of gifts of money, an action that is a violation of the constitutional provision.

Members of Ukpo community who were grown up by 1991, the year Dr. Walter Eze died would remember him as the foremost patriot and some would consider him the hero *per excellence* of the community. In 1957, Walter Eze returned to Nigeria from Canada where he qualified as a medical doctor. Ukpo was then a backwater community mostly unknown beyond its immediate area. The backwater status of Ukpo up to the 1950s can best be illustrated with the reaction of the people of Abagana after the court ruled the land case with them in favor of Ukpo. An official Abagana town crier announced to the members of that community that "ife di n'anadagbuluife di n'enu", i.e. the tail struck down the head. This lamentation which calls to mind the story of David and Goliath was in allusion to the situation which the people viewed as an incongruity of Ukpo a small and hitherto unknown community defeated Abagana that had been well known in Eastern Nigeria for a long time.

Ukpo is a small community compared with Abagana. In 1991, the population of Ukpo, approximately 14,000 was less than half the population of Abagana that was approximately 29,000[57]. Before Ukpo children started going to school, Abagana people had gone to school to become government officials beginning as domestic servants, messengers, etc. in the British colonial government establishment. From there Abagana people advanced to become top officials in the newly independent government of Eastern Nigeria beginning from the late 1950s to early 1960s. In fact by 1955, Ukpo children were still attending primary schools at Abagana. There were two primary schools in Ukpo, one was associated with the Anglican Church and the other with the Catholic Church but neither was complete. To complete primary school, Ukpo children had to go to Abagana until 1956 when the Anglican primary school in Ukpo community was upgraded to full primary school status.

Soon after he returned from Canada in 1957, Dr. Walter Eze established a hospital in Onitsha, an urban center about 30 km away from Ukpo. The hospital became the largest and most popular private hospital in Anambra state and perhaps in all of Eastern Nigeria. He organized several Ukpo people into a traders' cooperative society, funded the cooperative and made several people rich. He established a scholarship foundation in honor of his childhood friend who had died in an automobile accident and in so doing Walter Eze enabled several children of Ukpo community to go to school. He established a community maternity home which later became the Nnamdi Azikiwe University Teaching Hospital in Ukpo and he established the first secondary school in the community that was the Ukpo Girls' Secondary School. Walter Eze trained Arthur Eze, his junior brother who has continued his legacy of making considerable investments in the development of the town. As a result of Walter Eze's patriotic service

---

[57] The 1991 population census data were the latest census information published at the community level in Nigeria.

101

and sacrifice Ukpo became a well-known and respected community in Eastern Nigeria.

Since the year 2012, the town union had been funded virtually by one man, Arthur Eze, an arrangement that is unsustainable over time. The President General (2009 to 2011) rejected the voluntary contribution approach and opted for the compulsory levy approach and announced that he was putting measures in place to document the statistics that were necessary for that approach. But he did not get around to implementing the measures before the end of his term in 2011. His successor was neither interested in the compulsory levy nor in the voluntary contribution approach nor did he have any plan for fund raising.

The confusion of a parallel town union government that is exclusive for women resumed and internal feud returned to the women's wing after 2008. The action by the town union of 2006 to 2008 of co-opting women as members of the Central Executive, a measure that contained both problems is not sustained by succeeding town union governments. The confusion has continued to create tension among the women of the community. For example, in 2014 Arthur Eze gave money directly to the women's wing for the purpose of establishing cottage industries for the benefit of the women in the community. The women's wing could not manage the money because of internal acrimony. Some powerful members of the wing demanded that the chairperson surrender the money to them to manage. The town union government was powerless in resolving the conflict because the money was given directly to the women's wing independent of the Central Executive of the town union. The conflict escalated and resulted in arson in the town that culminated in the arrest of some of the women.

A few of the measures put in place by the town union government of 2006 to 2008 survived the sustainability concerns. Ban on all night noise with electronic public address systems generated from two sources, namely at funeral wake keeps and by church groups broadcasting their good messages was sustained to a good extent. The ban was sustained in the case of funeral wake keeps because it was convenient for the commercial operators. The ban allowed the commercial operators the opportunity to sleep without losing money because they were paid the same amount when they closed at 10.00 o'clock in the evening as when they closed at 05.00 o'clock in the morning.

The Opotor cultural festival continued to flourish in popularity. The popularity of the festival was being sustained by the Committee for the

Promotion of Culture in Ukpo; the association of non-Christians that were established in 2006; and by the personal interest in the festival shown by the traditional leader. The association of non-Christians in Ukpo has continued to grow in population. That association was self-sustaining by faith suggesting that there would be no basis for concern over its sustainability. Improved sanitation in public places was sustained to some extent because membership of the sanitation committee established in 2006 by the town union government of 2006 to 2008 was retained by subsequent town union government administrations. That committee has continued to carry out its functions.

To summarize, most of the people of Ukpo community would have liked that the various measures put in place by the town union government be maintained so that the achievements could be sustained. The town union institution does not have a bureaucracy and each President General comes with a new agenda. A few of the measures put in place by the town union government (2006 to 2008) survived that administration. For example, the revival of the major cultural festival of music and dance is sustained through promotion by two organizations established outside the context of the town union government but during its tenure and through the support of the traditional leader. Noise pollution control measure was sustained partially because commercial operators of electronic public address systems benefitted from the measure. Sanitation measures for public spaces are sustained to some extent because subsequent town union administrations retained the town union government (2006 to 2008) sanitation committee with its members who continued to function effectively.

CHAPTER ELEVEN

Summary of Interventions and Lessons

The community service that is reported in this book was implemented in Eastern Nigeria in Ukpo Dunukofia (hereafter Ukpo), a community that is in transition to an urban society following rapid economic growth in Nigeria and high population density in the area. In the Ukpo community a few well-to-do people and the poor masses share the same neighborhood. The impacts of relativity of poverty that result from that arrangement and the changed population dynamics elevate the rate and sophistication of crime as the poor see the possibilities of wealth in their neighborhoods and seek the opportunity, including for some people criminal opportunity, to acquire it. Private interests that are not checked in the society exploit communal interests. In the community this is manifested in terms of environmental abuse including random deforestation, noise pollution, and unhealthy disposal of wastes of all kinds.

Poor governance in Nigeria assure that basic living necessities such as in health, education, water and electricity supplies, roads, etc. are in poor states. Christian religion and western education erode the traditional cultural activities which anchor the existence of the people individually and communally. The impacts of all these deficiencies weigh heavily on the poor masses as the well-to-do are able to engage guards to secure their homes; have electricity generation plants and water boreholes in their homes; send their children to elite schools; and they have access to elite hospitals outside the community.

The community service was executed on the platform of a town union organization that came into being as an indigenous self-help community development organization in Igbo communities in Eastern Nigeria many years ago. Of recent, Igbo state governments in the country recognized the town unions as a democratic part, along with monarchy, of diarchy community governance without interfering with the self-help element by not providing subvention to the town unions. This exposed the town unions to the challenge of balancing its original feature, namely the self-help element with demands of urbanization that include expanded responsibilities with implication for increased budget needs of the town unions. Small size of territory under the control of the town union and the rural environment with mostly low income population imply that the revenue generation base is low for the town union government. High population pressure and increasing rate of commercialization in the area created additional challenge of intercommunity conflict that the town union had to face.

The community service provided in Ukpo during 2006 to 2008 period involved interventions in the areas of intercommunity conflict resolution, cultural revival, environmental protection, health, education, and security. The town union engaged in fund raising from among the members of the community and collaborated with bodies outside the community such as government agencies and an NGO to execute its interventions.

The conflicts between the Ukpo community and two neighboring communities were both settled in favor of Ukpo in court without violence in spite of manipulations of justice over more than 30 years by the Nigerian judiciary and in spite of provocations to violence by the opponents. The success was achieved through considerable sacrifice in terms of donations of money by some members of the community and by the determination of the people of Ukpo to pursue justice through legal rather than violent means. The faith of the people of Ukpo in a god that abhors bloodshed in the town was powerful in helping the course of non-violent settlement.

The impact of leadership of the town union in the area of cultural revival was mostly with respect to a traditional communal festival which competes with national festivals such as New Year, Easter, and Christmas for the interest of the members of the community and therefore, needed promotion to revive. The Central Executive of the town union voted against the town union government promoting the festival on the ground that it is a heathen festival. The President General organized a group of people independent of the town union to take responsibility for the promotion of the festival. The group which is supported by the traditional leader has been extremely successful and its effort is sustained.

Festivals that have parallels in the western world survived partially as they are still engaged in but without their traditional religious features. Cultural rites of passage such as marriage and funeral rites that are anchored on traditional faith survived the Christian evasion unscathed. Double standards in Christianity in the community found expression in the imperative, for the existence of the people, of the traditional rites of passage. Virtually every member of the community, Christians and non-Christians alike engages, overtly or covertly, in the performance of the heathen passage rites of marriage and funeral.

The abuse of the environment was in various forms including deforestation, noise pollution, and various forms of unsanitary life styles. The town union government was able to control to good extents deforestation, noise pollution, and some forms of unsanitary life styles by legislations that were rigorously enforced. The sanitation committee that was set up by the town union in 2006 is retained by subsequent town union administrations and that has helped to sustain part of the achievements in the area of sanitation. But the improved sanitation standard is only in relative terms as the town is still far from being a clean community. Ukpo cannot be an island on this matter, all over Africa unsanitary environment is the norm.

In 2006 orthodox health facilities in the community were meagre and in poor states. The education system was in need of financial support for the students, adequate number of qualified teachers, provision of school materials and equipment, and renovations of school buildings and sports facilities. Following solicitation by the town union government some members of the community helped especially in the areas of financial support for students and promotion of sporting activities in the schools. The town union was able to attract government investments that brought considerable improvements in both the health and education sectors in the community. While the state government was closing schools in the various communities in the state because of low enrollment, the same government established an additional secondary school in the community.

But the town union government could not change the poor state of the Nnamdi Azikiwe University Teaching Hospital in the community, such as deplorable state of medical records and the unprofessional practices of the hospital personnel especially the nurses who transfer their frustrations in form of lack of sympathy to patients. The nurses are over worked with low pay and do not have adequate equipment and materials for work. Some of the nurses entered the profession because they could not qualify or could not afford the training for the careers of their choice, mostly medicine and pharmacy.

The process of transition from rural to urban society brought a different dimension of crime in the community in terms of motive, sophistication, and frequency. Unlike before when the town was a

107

traditional village community, criminals now rob for the purpose of accumulating wealth. The robbers are now armed and they kill anybody that may stand on their way. Changed population dynamics following the process of urbanization helps to elevate the frequency of armed robbery in the community. The law enforcement unit of the town union, namely the Ukpo vigilante was poorly motivated with no financial remuneration and with minimum logistics support. Yet the force was able to serve as deterrent to criminals and the community was comparatively peaceful during the tenure of the town union government. The encouragement in the forms of revenue sharing and leadership by example that the town union government provided to the members of the vigilante force contributed to the success of the law enforcement unit of the town union.

Some of the numerous lessons that can be derived from the community development service are summarized. The process of transition from rural to urban society compounds the impact of poverty on the poor. Private interests of especially the powerful and the well-to-do members of the community transfer private costs to the community at high social costs. Deforestation for private purposes, mass advertisement by means of electronic public address systems, etc. mostly by the well-to-do have low private costs but their costs in terms of health hazards to the community, especially the poor masses are monumental.

Progressive leadership is central to the success of the town union in achieving its stated goals. A progressive leader is one who is more interested in making group members feel like leaders than in him/her being seen as the leader. The President General assigned responsibilities to members of the town union government and allowed them to take credit for their work. Courage, evenhandedness, selflessness, and compassion are virtues of leadership that worked in favor of the community service. Courage was required to pursue evenhandedness; without selflessness courage would lead to dictatorial governance that would be short in compassion. The President General's first target as his successor had courage but lacked selflessness; the second target possessed selfless attribute but did not measure up in courage.

Yoruba people of the South-West Nigeria call attention to the fate of retrogressive leaders in their communities with a metaphor, namely "Nineteen that would not associate with One has no chance of becoming Twenty" because leadership style impacts on the leader as it does on the people. When a leader lifts the people up by addressing their felt needs the people stand on his shoulders and hail him, he becomes taller by their height that is added to his. But if the leader steps down on the people, by embezzling their money for example, as the people struggle to get away they pull him down and he becomes a lesser person.

Faith is a powerful factor in the conduct of the affairs of the people of a community, it can lead to peaceful coexistence or it can create tensions in a community. To restrain restless young people who were eager to engage in violence in order to resolve the conflicts with neighboring communities, leaders of Ukpo community drew on, as a resource, the faith of the people in a deity that abhors bloodshed. On the other hand, the town union insistence on respect for all faiths including the heathen faith in the community led to the hostility of some Christian leaders towards the town union and that hostility caused much tension in the community.

Most of the achievements of the town union government demonstrate a lesson that interventions in the felt needs of the people have potentials for high payoff. For example, the intervention in the resolution of conflicts with two other communities proved effective because the people saw justice as imperative. The imperative motivated the people to support the intervention by voluntarily contributing money, ideas, and time towards the project. Similarly, Rural Women Foundation, an NGO operating in the community achieved considerable levels of success because its interventions were targeted directly to people in need, namely orphans and the vulnerable groups in the community.

The experiences of the interventions of the town union government in health and education systems demonstrate the power of self-help efforts in attracting outside support in a community. The modest self-help effort made by the town union government to improve the health facilities in the community by providing simple infrastructure for health posts attracted local government support in terms of providing a new health center and renovating the existing one in the community. Similarly the town union government efforts to improve the education system attracted state government attention to the extent that the state government increased the number of schools in the community when the same government was reducing the numbers of schools through merger because of low enrolment in other communities.

In the same way, active effort at collaboration with external bodies attracts investments from government and NGOs to a community such

109

as Ukpo. The high level of success achieved by the town union government in three years in the activity, i.e. collaborating with external bodies, which was led by a woman means that exclusion of women in town union governance is a mistake. Women make up half of the population and there is as much potential in them as in men for effective community governance.

Resource mobilization by the voluntary contribution approach worked because winning the two land cases with neighboring communities was a challenge seen as an imperative by members of the community. That reason was buoyed by the openness with which the finance of the community was handled. But the approach had a downside; the burden was borne by only a handful of the members of the community who are public spirited. Though most of such members were well-to-do, there were others who were also well-to-do but did not care. The challenge is to device an approach that would, without burdening the poor masses and without compromising the principle of self-help on which the town union institution was founded enable revenue generation on continuous and increasing basis. This is necessary because of the expanding responsibilities of the town union institution under the process of transition from rural to urban society. The town union institution in Ukpo community should under-study the experiences of town union governments in communities in the area that have progressed further in the transition process.

Confirmation of most of the concerns for sustainability of the accomplishments of the town union government would not be surprising considering the boldness of some of the actions and considering that those actions are meant to deny people including powerful people the lifestyle that they are used to. What is surprising is that the people who are expected to help sustain the achievements are among the ones that abused the various measures put in place by the town union government. Some of those people played key roles in the town union governance and therefore, helped to put the measures in place. But more importantly, the various interventions were not sustained because although through frequent re-election of the members of the town union government the town union organization should have strong institutional memory but it has no bureaucracy and each President General comes on board with his own agenda.

APPENDIX I

Yes, I Accept to Serve as President General Ukpo Improvement Union[58]

Felix Nweke
(Ichie Ozozuluigbon'Ukpo)

Your Royal Highness, Igwe (Dr.) Robert C. Eze, Okofia the Sixth, Eze Ukpo, Dunukofia; fellow members of the Igwe Robert's cabinet; religious leaders; members of the UIU (Ukpo Improvement Union) Central Executive; President Generals Silvanus Nwako, Silvanus Anika, Anthony Ezekwesili, and Gibson Okeke; Secretary General NwankwoIgweilo; Nzen'Ozo; Umu Okpu and Ndi Inyom; Uzodinma Age Grade; and Ladies and Gentlemen.

I received a call from the people of Akaezi village to serve, on their behalf as the President General of Ukpo Improvement Union for the period 2006 to 2008 with the assurance that nobody was interested in taking up the responsibility. I consulted with close friends and associates such as Bertram Okpokwasili II, Samuel Ifeacho, among others all of whom told me that it was an important and necessary obligation. I did not present myself at the Igwe's 2005 Yam Festival as is required of a candidate who was nominated by his village because I did not want to influence decision on my confirmation.

All along as I pondered over the request by my village two factors kept bugging my mind. Thought of three recent deaths in Akaezi, namely those of Edwin Nweke, Patrick Okoye and Christopher Nwafor was heavy in my mind. Edwin Nweke and Patrick Okoye were pre-eminent leaders in Akaezi and Christopher Nwafor would have been a more appropriate candidate than me to serve as the President General on behalf of Akaezi village was he to be alive today[59]. The second factor that was weighing heavily on my mind is the debt I owe the town as a whole for the part the people played in my upbringing; service as President General would be an opportunity for me to give back to the community.

---

[58] English translation of the inaugural address presented in Igbo language at the Ukpo convention on December 29, 2005.
[59] Christopher Nwafor had retired from regular job.

So here I am presenting an acceptance speech; yes, I shall serve the people of Ukpo in the capacity as President General for the next three years to the best of my ability. There are two points that I need to raise upfront. The UIU will not protect sacred cows; under my leadership everybody is under the law. The second point is that everybody's God or gods must be respected. My grandmother used to quote someone she called Sarah who was half god and half human. On Oye market days, Sarah would walk about in the market square repeatedly saying to no one in particular "Onyena Chie Onyena Chie" meaning mind your god or God and leave others with theirs. This statement of Sarah which I personally consider a wise admonition will guide the UIU under my charge.

I appreciate the efforts of the outgoing UIU and those of others before it. In my judgement they performed exceedingly well under their respective circumstances. Yet looking around it is easy to see that outstanding needs of the people are many and serious. The environment is being racked through unrestrained deforestation, noise pollution, indecent and unhygienic lifestyles because private interests are left unchallenged to exploit communal interests at high social costs. Culture that anchors the people individually and communally is being eroded by western civilization and urbanization. I do not need to dwell on the appalling states of education of our children, health, electricity and water supplies, the so called amenities because they are well known problematic areas in our country as a whole.

In my judgment Ukpo has not shown sufficient appreciation of the people who served the community with all they had, we forget too soon. We ought to commemorate our heroes so that people will aspire to serve the community. There are many heroes that need to be commemorated but one is uppermost in my mind, namely Walter Eze. No doubt, Walter Eze stands out as the foremost patriot and some will consider him the hero per excellence of the community. In 1957, the year Walter Eze returned from Canada where he qualified as a medical doctor, Ukpo was a backwater community mostly unknown beyond its immediate area.

Soon after he returned from Canada, Walter Eze organized several people into Oranto Brothers Traders' Cooperative Society, funded the cooperative and made several people rich. He established a scholarship foundation in honor of his childhood friend, Eugene Ezulu who had died in a motor accident and in so doing he enabled several children of Ukpo community to go to school. He established a community maternity home which is now the Nnamdi Azikiwe University Teaching Hospital in Ukpo and he established the first secondary school in the community. Walter Eze trained Arthur Eze who continues to make considerable investments in the development of the town. As a result of Walter Eze's patriotic service and sacrifice, Ukpo became a well-known and respected community in Eastern Nigeria. Walter Eze died 14 years ago; this is the time to do something to commemorate his life, not for him but for generations of Ukpo people to come.

All those are important areas for intervention but we must prioritize because of limited resources. I believe that almost all of us will agree that the two land disputes, one between Ukpo and Abba and the other between Ukpo and Abagana together ought to constitute the number one priority for the incoming UIU because they place our territorial integrity and therefore, our existence as a community on the balance. The court cases on both have been lying dormant for a number of years now. With default consent by Ukpo people, Abba people have been comfortable enjoying the injustice against us granted them by Mr. Ononiba, namely the indefinite stay of execution of the justice which we earned. This will stop.

The incoming UIU will reactivate both cases and pursue them with all-out determination. In doing that, the incoming UIU re-affirms the long standing approach by Ukpo, namely abhorrence of violent approach to the solution of both problems. Ukpo's position of non-violence approach stands on two powerful grounds, namely Ukpo has *Ajana* which harbors repugnancy against bloodshed and Ukpo aims at peace as ultimate goal while bloodshed will make peace more difficult to achieve. We therefore, invite both Abba and Abagana people to commit to the ideal of non-violent solution because no matter who wins in the disputes, victory will be lost without peace. Let us settle the disputes in court; Ukpo will be patient with legal approach with the firm trust that justice will prevail.

I have on behalf of the incoming UIU enumerated what we consider as priority issues that need attention in the next three years. How much the UIU can do depends on how much support you, the members of the community can provide. How much we can do also depends on your patience and understanding because facing the enumerated challenges has implications for sacrifice in different forms by the people and therefore, calls for patience and understanding.

I thank all of you for listening.

113

APPENDIX II

Mutual Respect among Leadership Institutions in Ukpo[60]
By Felix Nweke
President General
Ukpo Improvement Union

Introduction

Your Royal Highness, Igwe (Dr) Robert C. Eze, Okofia VI, Eze Ukpo; Ndi Ichie (herein Cabinet); members of the Central Executive Committee of the Ukpo Improvement Union (hereafter UIU). What I am going to tell you today were not discussed with the UIU. What I am about to say represent my personal view, which is borne out of my experience as the President General of the Ukpo Improvement Union for the past 12 months. What I have in mind are of critical importance to Ukpo and everyone needs to pay attention.

An Act of Disrespect

At the present time, Ukpo is facing a very tough situation so much that leaders cannot afford to make any mistake no matter how small. The situation is like "Omembu, malu" because "Omeiboo" is fatally too late. Yet two weeks ago today on Saturday December 2, 2006, the Cabinet at Ukpo passed a law to reintroduce the ban on all private celebrations from December 15 to January 1 each holiday season. This, the Cabinet did without reference to the UIU. Yet the UIU is expected to endorse if not to enforce it. I consider this an act of disrespect by the Cabinet for the UIU and I condemn it.

How did I learn about this action of the Cabinet? On the same day, December 2, 2006, the UIU held a meeting until late in the evening as usual, and again as usual I went to the Igwe, to brief him on the outcome of the UIU meeting. That was when Ichie Oranyelu Eze informed the Igwe, not me, that the Cabinet had resolved to reintroduce the ban. The

---

[60] An address presented to the joint meeting of the members of the Igwe's Cabinet and the members of the Central Executive Committee of the Ukpo Improvement Union at the Igwe's Palace on Saturday December 16, 2006.

Igwe, the Ide and Ichie Oji Udo promptly stopped action on this law following my complaint. On behalf of the people of Ukpo, I thank the three of them; I also thank Ichie Oranyelu Eze who did not mind mentioning it to my hearing. The Cabinet would have received a shock because the reaction of the UIU would have been unexpected. These four citizens have saved Ukpo from a disaster of polarization that would have followed this act had the Cabinet carried through with it.

Why should have the UIU reacted drastically to this Cabinet action of lack of respect? The answer is that the UIU wishes to be seen as an institution, which respects, but not subservient, to sister institutions such as the Cabinet. How many times have the UIU presented proposals to make law to the Cabinet? I ask, do you think that it was done out of weakness by the UIU? Certainly, not; the UIU consulted because it is the right thing to do.

Let me tell you how far the UIU consults! A few weeks ago, Prof Chinyere Okunna asked the UIU to give her two names of Ukpo undergraduates to receive the Admora-Okunna Foundation University scholarship for the current academic year. The UIU went to the UUU (Ukpo Undergraduate Union) for consultation. Why not? We could easily nominate the candidates but we considered that a little involvement of the UUU would give the young people a sense of belonging. It is a matter of respect, if you give someone respect you get the best out of him.

A UIU that is conceived by Ukpo people as weak, a UIU, which has no mind of its own, a UIU, which is dictated to by anybody including the Cabinet will kill Ukpo, dead! It is the responsibility of all of us to create the image of a strong and independent UIU for the benefit of Ukpo people. Rather than compete for supremacy with the UIU, the Cabinet has the responsibility to encourage the UIU to perform at its best.

Let everybody including the Cabinet put the ego behind so that we can work together as equals as we face the serious challenges of today. Today is not the right time to talk about who is under whom, Cabinet or UIU; all of us are equal under Ukpo.

Changing the Law on Private Celebrations

Igwe, let me address this law which your Cabinet attempted to reintroduce by a unilateral action. First of all, there must not be any change in this law this holiday season December 15, 2006 to January 1,

2007 because it is too late in the day. Change for subsequent seasons is a subject of discussion by the UIU and the Cabinet on an equal basis. My personal view on the matter is that today is not the time to change a law that does no harm to Ukpo. The reason is that "Onyeokunaagbabieanachurooke".

Today, Ukpo is waging legal battles with belligerent neighbors in more than one front. Each of these battles has the potential of producing a consequence similar to a physical battle. For example, a loss of the legal battle in the Abba front ("Ana ekwena") would certainly mean that in order to continue to exist as a town, Ukpo will have to pay ransom to Abba. I ask all of you, who among us will like to live to see this happen?

"Ana ekwena" means that those of us who are privileged to be leaders today must put our personal interests, including our ego, aside and work together as respectful equals in order to guarantee that the unacceptable result does not arise. We are Ichies and Cabinet and all that only as privileged people. There are many who deserve the Ichie title as much if not more than any one of us. But they are not, many because they do not want and others because they are not discovered. Is Miss Universe the most beautiful woman in the world? Certainly not, she is the most beautiful only among a few scores who present themselves for competition.

The Law on Use of Public Address System

Let me address a different but closely related matter. On the same December 2, 2006, I consulted the Igwe on the UIU proposal to suspend the law banning the use of public address system after 10.00 pm from December 20 to January 1 in order to accommodate the Ofala festival. The Igwe pointed out to me that that law is a popular law which guarantees residents a restful night after each day's work; suspension might weaken it. The Igwe further pointed out to me that although that law originated from the UIU it was endorsed by the Cabinet. If suspension weakens the law, Ukpo people will blame both the UIU and the Cabinet.

The Igwe also pointed out that the Ofala is a UIU festival; both the UIU and the Cabinet signed the invitation. He noted that the invitation was distributed to several friends of Ukpo; if such people enjoy themselves beyond 10.00 pm it would be impolite to ask them to leave. After these convincing explanations, I immediately instructed the

117

UIU authorities to suspend action. Messers Ifeaka Nwachala and Emma Nwankwo, the Secretary General and Public Relations Manager respectively of the UIU, you now know the reason for my instruction. I hereby invite Ukpo people and their friends worldwide to come out and enjoy the Ofala because it is their festival. But I advise that the use of public address system after 10.00 pm is limited to December 22 and 23 at the Igwe's palace and Arthur's residence where the Ofala is also celebrated. Any use of public address system outside these dates and locations is a violation of this Ukpo popular law.

I thank you all for your attention.

APPENDIX III

Dividends of Progressive Leadership in Ukpo[61]
By
Felix Nweke
President General
Ukpo Improvement Union

Your Royal Highness, Igwe (Dr) Robert C. Eze Okofia the Sixth, Eze Ukpo; fellow members of the Igwe Robert's cabinet; all the Igwes of Dunukofia and other Igwes; special guests; religious leaders; members of the UIU (Ukpo Improvement Union) Central Executive; President Generals Silvernus Nwako, Silvernus Anika, Anthony Ezekwesili, and Gibson Okeke; Secretary Generals NwankwoIgweilo and Ifeaka Nwachala, Umu Okpu, Ndi Inyom, members of Uzodinma age grade ladies and gentlemen. I thank all of you for honoring our invitation to today's event.

Introduction

Igwe, about four decades ago in the mid-1960s (seems like yesterday) at Nsukka, you and I and others such as Herbert Okonkwo (Ichie Oji Udo) were concerned with passing our "something-0-something" examinations. We were sheltered from the hard realities of leadership at Ukpo by such giant patriots as Michael Eze, Nathaniel Okeke, Walter Eze, Fredrick Eze Nwankwo Igweilo, Benson Okoye, Augustine Esedo, Silvernus Nwako, etc. I wonder if at that time you predicted that someday the leadership of the town would fall on your shoulders. Certainly, I did not think that today I shall be in the position of the President General of the UIU (Ukpo Improvement Union) assisting you in the tough role of providing leadership at Ukpo, especially now that the town is facing various challenges including the unprovoked assault on our territorial integrity by an alliance of certain neighboring towns.

The challenges of our time are essentially the same as those of our

---

[61] An address presented on behalf of the UIU (Ukpo Improvement Union) to H. R. H. Igwe (Dr) Robert C. Eze, Okofia the Sixth, Eze Ukpo on the occasion of his fifteenth Ofala Festival.

predecessors: an assault on the territorial integrity of the town; poor infrastructure such as inadequate water and power supplies, and poor road network; mass poverty which denies our children the right to proper education and our elderly the right to adequate medical care and nutrition; among others. The difference is that these challenges are more intense today than before because of increased population pressure. Fortunately, we have progressive leadership, which you provide.

Progressive Leadership at Ukpo

Igwe, I want to underline progressive leadership because it is a reality at Ukpo. I can name towns around whose citizens abroad are reluctant to visit home because they do not want to see their Igwe. In contrast, Ukpo citizens abroad come home regularly and you are aware of the large number of them who touch base with you. What you may not know is that when they return to their places of residence, they report with pride that they spoke to the Igwe.

Igwe, your case is an excellent illustration that progressive leadership inspires mass followership. As soon as your high level of integrity and commitment to courses, which are good for Ukpo were understood, Ukpo people worldwide came out in large numbers to support the UIU programs with their expertise, time and money. Several of them put their lives on the line in order to help secure what belongs to Ukpo. I have heard it said that "igwebuike" at Ukpo because the expertise, time and money contributions are made without prodding. In the year under review, 2006, the UIU did not levy citizens compulsorily to implement its programs. Rather several citizens donated freely whatever they could to the various UIU courses.

Ukpo has become a training ground for leadership. That one does not have to be the Igwe or a President General in order to be a leader has become a popular slogan at Ukpo. Ukpo citizens now voluntarily stand guard day and night in order to protect Ukpo interests. In Lagos, under the budding leadership of Emmanuel Otunabor the UIU Youth Wing is emerging. Also emerging is the UUU (Ukpo Undergraduates Union) under the calm and calculated leadership of Izuchukwu Nwabueze. A group of women call themselves the Dancing Queens of Ukpo as they organize a cultural troupe under the powerful leadership of Amaka Ezeabulunne-Okweleze. You are aware that from November 22 to 27, this year an Ukpo masquerade cultural troupe, namely Nwamkpa led by Chiedu Omeleke and Peter Adibe represented Anambra State at a national cultural event in Abuja.

UIU branches are thriving under vibrant leaderships: North America branch, led by Anthony Adubasim; Lagos, Levi Abalogu; Onitsha, Raphael Akude; and Port Harcourt, Boniface Okoye. These are a few of the UIU branches which are doing very well because of progressive leadership. Julius Anika Jnr, single handedly founded the Ukpo International Forum, a venue where Ukpo citizens worldwide debate issues of common interest. At Ukpo, the traditionalists are mobilizing under the leadership of NwoyeOdah and Eric Omejilichi. These die-hard traditionalists seem determined to rake up from the dust and keep alive Ukpo traditional religion and culture which help to sustain all of us.

Igwe, you can easily see from the above analysis that young citizens of Ukpo are taking advantage of your progressiveness to realize their leadership potentials. I have a vision, Ukpo is about to produce top private and public sector leaders not only for Nigeria but for the world at large. Without question, progressive leadership is everything for good governance.

UIU Activities in 2006

On December 29, 2005 at the Oye market square, the UIU unveiled its program for the following three years. Among the projects outlined, security of the Ukpo territory was the number one priority. In 2006, with strong backing of the Concerned Citizens of Ukpo and the Ukpo Security Council, the UIU took on the security problem with a deserved attention. In so doing, we were guided by your counsel, which is that in the face of violent provocations by our aggressive neighbors we must continue to seek redress only in the law courts in order to resolve our differences with them. I complement our lawyers and other friends of Ukpo who support us in our effort to secure what is ours.

In the year under review, 2006, several activities which were not in our plan but which could not wait such as the national population census, voters' registration and quantification of the erosion problem at Ukpo engaged the UIU attention. But because of the over-riding importance of the security problem, the UIU did not devote attention to other important concerns including education.

The rehabilitation of the electricity facility at Ukpo was embarked on because the ground work for it was completed earlier by Prince Arthur

Eze. The rehabilitation was planned to be completed by the end of this month, December 2006. Unfortunately, the boss of the contracting company handling the work was involved in the Sokoto flight disaster. The rehabilitation is funded by the Federal Government at a cost of 63 million Naira. We are grateful to the Prince Arthur Eze for initiating the project. We are also grateful to Anthony Ezekwesili who followed to maturation the request to the Federal Government for this project.

Road is one of the most important infrastructures for economic development. Ukpo had already expressed gratitude to Governor Ngige for the construction of the Otimgbodomgbo road. But the construction was shoddy and UIU petition is now on the desk of the Anambra State Governor. It is expected that the state government will not make further payment to the contracting firm, i.e. Master Holdings Nig Ltd until that road is properly done. The Abagana-Ukpo-Abba-IfiteDunu-Awkuzu road is begging for reconstruction because it is no longer motorable.

Announcements

All of us will benefit from the construction of the EziOraja-Oye-Ezi Eze road done by Prince Arthur Eze. Prof. Chinyere Okunna renewed the Adimora-Okunna Foundation scholarship for Ukpo citizens at both the secondary and university levels. The UIU has already sent her an acknowledgement message.

In the year under review, several Ukpo citizens attained major accomplishments in terms of promotions in places of work, appointments to leadership positions, and recognition awards. Among these are Ifeanyi Omeokachie who bagged the national merit award of MFR (Member of the Order of the Federal Republic); Chinyere Okunna, appointed the Commissioner for Information and Culture, Anambra State Government; and Samuel Okeke, promoted as Director in the NNPC (Nigerian National Petroleum Corporation). Eric Okoye was honored by the UIU North America branch for long term commitment to the security and development of Ukpo. Ukpo citizens bagged Ph D degrees some of which were in high technology sciences from world renowned universities.

Ukpo lost several citizens to death among who are Gideon Nweke Otubelu, Bishop Emeritus Enugu Anglican Communion and Priscilla Ifediba Anika, Mother of Faith. The UIU participated in the funerals as necessary.

Looking Ahead

Looking ahead to the coming year, we note that problem of the threat to the security of our territory is not yet resolved. In the coming year, the UIU will pursue that problem with re-enforced vigor. In fact, the UIU is not in a hurry over this matter, we will continue to press on no matter the cost in terms of time, money and other resources. But Igwe, I assure you that the UIU will continue to heed your wise counsel, i.e. to shun violence because in the end in order to sustain victory, peace must also be won. Peace with Abba is important to Ukpo because between the two towns a river of common blood runs swell; that is also true with respect to Abagana.

Acknowledgements

In the year under review, 2006, more than ever before, several Ukpo citizens made their money available to support UIU programs. Some of the contributions per person were quite large. The UIU circulated income account regularly, anyone wishing to see who contributed what should consult those periodic accounts. But UIU is grateful to all those who made those contributions.

The cooperation of the Igwe's cabinet with the UIU in arriving at various decisions and implementing different programs in the year under review was maximal. Ukpo people are the beneficiaries of this cooperation which guarantees that the decisions and the actions of the UIU are right and durable.

The public officers assigned to Ukpo and to the Dunukofia LGA (Local Government Area) deserve our applause. The various church leaders, school teachers, officers of the National Population Commission, Independent National Election Commission, Nigerian Agriculture and Cooperative Bank, the Nnamdi Azikiwe University Teaching Hospital, the various law enforcement agencies among others worked as if they forgot that they were Nigerian public servants.

Ukpo has special friends among who are Gen Ibrahim Babangida and Ambassador Uche Okeke. These special relationships are highly appreciated.

I salute you who will today be coronated Ukpo Chiefs. Ukpo chieftaincy is a serious matter; it is given for service rendered to mankind anywhere in the world. The bearer is under obligation to comport himself or herself properly and in particular to have courage to stand by what he sees and always stand on the side of truth.

Igwe, I have reserved the last mention for the greatest, Price Arthur Eze whom the UIU coroneted as "Ebube Ukpo" in the year under review. The existence *per se* of the Prince is protective of Ukpo. Besides whenever the going gets tough we always have the Prince to fall back on. Igwe, this address, which is on behalf of the UIU is for your attention, but please let me address the Prince briefly.

Prince Arthur Eze, it took me one year as President General of the UIU to arrive at an important realization, namely that one smart action by you at a critical point in the recent history of Ukpo saved the town from atrophy. Without that single action Ukpo would today be a town without energy whose citizens work with heads cast down than up. May your sun shine for many more years.

Igwe, at Ukpo things do not happen randomly, things are guided to happen.

That is all I have for you today, I thank you for your attention.

Copied to:
1. The heads of all mainline Churches at Ukpo
2. Principals of all secondary schools at Ukpo
3. Head Masters/ Mistresses of all primary schools at Ukpo
4. Head teachers of all nursery schools at Ukpo

APPENDIX IV

Self-Determined Cultural Imperialism: A Drag on Progress[62]
Felix Nweke[63]
President General
Ukpo Improvement Union

Your Royal Highness, IgweDr Robert C Eze, Okofia the Sixth, Eze Ukpo; Ndi Ichie n'Ukpo; Ndi Igwe Dunukofia; all NdiIgwe, all Ndi Ichie; all Nzena Ozo; Ndi Ezenwanyi, Umu Abo, Umu Okpu; Umu Ada; NdiInyom; Special Guests; Friends of Ukpo; Ladies and Gentlemen.

Introduction

Igwe, the UIU (Ukpo Improvement Union) takes the opportunity of your Ofala festival to bring you up to date on the state of the town over which you reign by reviewing the events of the past 12 months. Self-determined cultural imperialism has a negative connotation but it can be analyzed to summarize major events of the year under review (December 24, 2006 to December 22, 2007). This point will be illustrated by reporting on the progress of the UIU program including accomplishments and acknowledgements of people who provided the support leading up to those accomplishments.

Self-Determined Cultural Imperialism

In the year under review, self-determined cultural imperialism constituted a formidable but surmountable problem against the attainment of the UIU goals aimed at social justice, a system under which people do not exploit one another. Colonial domination is a Nigerian heritage; the colonialists imposed foreign and unfamiliar culture, which they considered superior to the indigenous one. People's response varied,

---

[62] An address on behalf of the UIU (Ukpo Improvement Union) to HRH IgweDr R C Eze, Okofia VI, Eze Ukpo on the occasion of his 16th Ofala Festival on December 22, 2007 in Dunukofia Palace, Ukpo, Dunukofia.

[63] Felix Nweke (Ichie Ozozuluigbon'Ukpo) was a Professor of Agricultural Economics, University of Nigeria, Nsukka. He is a Visiting Professor of African Studies and Institute of International Agriculture, Michigan State University, East Lansing, Michigan 48823, USA.

some aspects of the foreign culture were uncritically accepted in blind obedience while others were resisted, in some cases in the form of cowardly sabotage and in other cases through bold civil disobedience. These modes of resistance were necessary and viable survival strategies for a people who were cowed by the superior colonial power. But carried forward to the present, the modes of resistance present formidable obstacles to progress towards social justice. Igwe, in obedience to your instruction to keep this address brief I shall analyze the role of uncritical acceptance of a foreign culture in order to illustrate the problem posed to the UIU by self-determined cultural imperialism.

Without question, Ukpo people accept the Christian culture and civilization, which offer obvious advantages. Since its introduction in Ukpo in the second decade of the twentieth century, Christianity has spiritually sustained and nourished thousands of people by providing them hope and meaning for life.

It is easy for an impartial observer to see that in Ukpo the Christian and the indigenous traditional cultures are gradually progressing towards convergence. The celebrations of New Year, Opoto, Easter, New Yam, and Christmas festivals by Christians and non-Christians in the community are vivid manifestations of this dynamic process. Similarly, the dual celebrations of the key stages in human life cycle such as marriages, births and deaths in some cases with similar kinds of rituals by both the Christians and the traditional faith people signify progress towards the convergence of the two cultures. While people in one of the two major religious traditions in Ukpo urge the process on as a marriage which can give birth to something new and beautiful, some central figures in the other tradition vilify it as satanic, which needs urgent battle to contain.

In Ukpo, certain groups within one of the religious traditions define themselves in some kind of tension with the rest of the people. With their action, they make clear their determination to be above the constitution of the town. In other words their intention is to exist in Ukpo but not conform to the laws. The danger posed to the program of the UIU by the group inspired by or operating under the guise of a foreign culture is clear; the role of such a group is a catalyst for civil disobedience and the collapse of the UIU programs.

The UIU Programs: A Progress Report

In the year under review (December 24, 2006 to December 22, 2007), the UIU continued from where it stopped to implement measures aimed at enthroning social justice in the town. First priority remained the security of property against hostile neighbors. We have continued to pursue this priority by seeking justice through the law courts because we understand that no alternative will enthrone social justice in the society. We are doing this with a great deal of patience.

Education is another priority sector. In the year under review the Education Committee of the UIU under the chairmanship of Godson Ofora produced a report which named the various problems plaguing the public education system in the town. The UIU started to implement measures aimed at remedying some of those problems.

Ukpo has three public secondary schools renamed in the year under review as Community Secondary School, Ukpo; Walter Eze Memorial Secondary School, Ukpo; and Dunukofia High School, Ukpo. Two of the dilapidated buildings in these schools were rehabilitated one in the Community Secondary School, Ukpo by the state government through the intervention of Chinyere Okunna and the other in Dunukofia High School, Ukpo by the Ukpo Youth League of the UIU Lagos branch. Also through Chinyere Okunna's intervention, the state government provided a borehole at the Community Secondary School, Ukpo.

There are four public primary schools in Ukpo; Central School, Obioma, Aguafor and Unity. Again two of the dilapidated buildings in the primary schools were renovated with matching funds provided by the state government and some Ukpo people one in the Central School and the other in Aguafor. A befitting security fence was erected at the Central School by Arthur Eze.

A new development in the education system in Ukpo was introduced in the year under review as part of the AIM (AIDS Impact Mitigation) project funded in Nigeria by the USAID (United States Agency for International Development) and implemented in Ukpo by the Rural Women Foundation. The AIM project is implemented in six Nigerian states with one project site such as Ukpo in each of the six states. The AIM project aims to improve the quality of life of HIV infected individuals and their families and to provide support to orphans and vulnerable children, particularly the girl-child. In the year under review the AIM project organized a training program for 40 widows of HIV

127

victims on alternative micro business enterprise possibilities and on profit and loss accounting. The project provided the widows the sum of 12,000 Naira each to start micro businesses.

The AIM project also organized evening classes for 40 orphans whose parents were HIV victims. The children were provided with bright school uniforms including tops, pants or skates and sandals and school bags as well as books, paper and pencils. The children are offered classes five days a week; they receive milk and 20 Naira each school day. Chuma Ezedinma made possible the coming to Ukpo of this project of compassion, which will unfortunately end in October 2008.

In the year under review, the health facilities in Ukpo increased in number, health centers from one to two and health posts from one to five. The dramatic increases were accomplished through the effort of the UIU Health Committee under the chairmanship of Elias Okafor.

One other important area of focus of effort by the UIU is cultural revival. The unprecedented high level of participation by Ukpo people and their friends in the 2007 Opoto festival leaves no one in doubt that the people approve the high UIU priority rating for cultural revival in the town.

People of the Omenana faith are now well organized under the leaderships of Eric Omejilichi and Nwamgbede Ajagu. The group holds regular meetings and they support one another especially psychologically during occasions of severe emotional stress such as deaths and funerals. Today in Ukpo, men and women, old and young in large numbers confess their traditional faith holding their heads high with deserved pride. This development is of a fundamental importance for the increasing number of people who no longer find spiritual anchor in the more popular faith traditions in the town.

Igwe, the present UIU introduced six bylaws since inception in the areas of sanitation, noise control, environmental protection, and revenue collection. The bylaws aim at enthroning social justice, a system under which people do not exploit one another. Exploitation of the poor by the rich easily comes to mind, but the more pervasive and by far the more detrimental to the noble value of social justice is the abuse of communal interests by private individuals, rich or poor.

Examples abound: encroaching on communal lands; dumping of human waste, household refuse, and farm residues into the streets; channeling of sewage or soakaway or flood into the streets; and operating loud public address systems late into the night. Another example is stopping a vehicle in the middle of the road to greet, to load, to off load while keeping other drivers waiting. All these are done with a total abandonment of simple courtesy. They constitute social injustice because they abuse communal interests.

Acknowledgements

The easiest part of this address in terms of composing it is the acknowledgement because many patriots by their generosity offered themselves to be acknowledged. The only difficult part is deciding which of the generous people can be excluded to save on volume. To attempt to resolve this dilemma I shall acknowledge some people in groups; first the Eze family of Ukpo, Dunukofia. Since I grew up in the 1950s and 1960s, my experience of Ukpo has been parallel with my experience of the Eze family from Michael Anaekwe Eze through Walter and Fredrick Eze to Robert and Arthur Eze. The experiences are not only in name as when one thinks of Ukpo one thinks of the Eze family and *vice versa*. The experience is in more concrete and substantial terms such as the defense of Ukpo interests and more recently investments in the economic empowerment of the residents of the town. Why is the above the case? Why does the Eze family invest so much in Ukpo? The significance of these questions is illuminated by removing Royal and viewing the Eze family simply as an Ukpo family. Even then, the Eze family has suffered because rather than appreciate the family's generosity, several Ukpo people misinterpret it.

The good news is that most members of the Eze family seem not perturbed; their patience seems inexhaustible. The family continues to give because they seem to understand that what one has one is given to share. In the year under review alone, Arthur invested well over one hundred million Naira on the welfare of Ukpo in the reconstruction of the Oye Market square, renovation of churches and schools, scholarships, repair and maintenance of roads, sinking boreholes, landscaping of major roads in the town, setting up a water purification industry for rural employment generation and free distribution of money to the poor. As the Eze family continues to give they continue to increase in fortune.

A town is known for its unique attributes, Ukpo is gradually developing attributes peculiar to it and not duplicated in other rural towns. Street lighting and landscape architecture are now unique

129

attributes of Ukpo. Arthur has made a firm promise to build, in the coming year, monuments in honor of three great leaders and patriots of Ukpo in order to provide true landmarks in the town.

Close collaboration and cordial working relationship between the UIU and the Igwe-in-Council can only be described in superlative terms. That collaboration assures that the UIU decisions and programs are objective and durable. Igwe, without doubt, the close and cordial working relationship between the two leadership institutions is owed to the progressive leadership which you provide as I discussed in this forum a year ago.

My colleagues in the UIU Central Executive and in the branches deserve to be acknowledged. The objective decisions and action programs of the UIU which they implemented required unparalleled commitment. Chinyere Okunna, Paul Okeke, Chris Ayolugbe, Eric Udemba, Chuma Ezedinma, Eric Omejilichi, Herbert Okonkwo, Okwuchukwu Ezeaku, Bertram Okpokwasili, Emma Ekee and many more deserve acknowledgement.

Announcements

Oye Ukpo market square was rebuilt completely with long span roofs and concrete interlocking flour, solid drainage and sanitation facilities solely by Arthur Eze. Arthur also provided several millions of Naira for the renovation of St Mary's Anglican Church building and gave large sums of money to sum other churches in the town.

Chinyere Okunna renewed the Adimora Okunna Foundation scholarship and increased the number of beneficiaries from three last year to eight this year. The All Saints Anglican Church building construction is in progress in Akpu village. St Joseph's Catholic Church in Aguafor is struggling to complete the residence of its priest. That young church needs help from people of good heart who have the spirit of giving. The Christian faith tradition plays positive role in the society because, as other faith traditions, it provides community and spiritual anchor for believers. Ukpo people should continue to provide financial support to the churches.

The 2007 national voter registration returned a figure of over 22,000 voting age, 18 years and above, population for Ukpo, a reflection of the demographic status of the town. The UIU committee for the national voters' registration under the chairmanship of Vincent Ilora and large financial commitment by Paul Okeke assured that Ukpo people came out in large numbers to register and therefore assured accurate counting.

In the year under review, the UIU began implementing its documentation program and published the maiden edition of the Ukpo-Dunukofia Calendar of Events, Culture and Tourism. The UIU produced master copies of audios and videos of the Ayaka, Anyafulugo, and a rendition by St Mary's Anglican Church choir. Publication and marketing of the audios and videos are awaiting availability of funds.

Ukpo leadership has continued to promote gender equality; two women now sit in the UIU Central Executive as co-opted members. Several women, indigenes and non-indigenes, are Ukpo Chiefs. Their number will today swell with the coronation shortly of Mrs Eunice Okpokwasili as Chief Amalunwezen'Ukpo. The Anyafulugo women's cultural dance group under the leadership of Mrs Amaka Ezeabulunne-Okweleze is making waves flying Ukpo flag in distant places. In the year under review the Anyafulugo cultural dance group of Ukpo represented Dunukofia three times at different state cultural events in Awka and represented Anambra State in the national carnival last month. Mrs. Amaka Ezeabulunne-Okweleze organized this great cultural troupe last year.

Now the sad news, death was rampant in the town in the year under review. Ukpo lost many people including three Ichies namely Ezedinma, Ekwulu I and Chineme. Ukpo also lost other prominent people such as John Mezue, Shedrack Ifedili, Oswald Okonkwo, etc.

Looking Ahead

In the next one year, I do not see what the UIU would do differently except intensifying already intensive efforts towards the goals of social justice, a system under which people do not exploit one another. Security of the territory of Ukpo remains number one priority and the means to that goal remains justice through the law court. Cultural revival is critical because Cosmos Ezulu counsels that in the absence of our culture we will not recognize our birth rights. Education, health and other aspects of economic empowerment remain paramount on the priority list. The present UIU is gearing for a final push on these priority programs as it enters its third and final year which begins on December 29 this year. The UIU is confident in expecting continued support by all Ukpo patriots.

Igwe, I stop here and thank everybody for listening.

APPENDIX V

A Call from Home to Serve[64]

Felix Nweke
President General
Ukpo Improvement Union

Preamble

Your Royal Highness, Igwe Dr R. C. Eze, Okofia VI, Eze Ukpo; Igwe-In-Council; Dunukofia Igwes; other Traditional Rulers and Leaders, Your Excellencies; Chairman of ASATU (Dr I. I. Onwubuya); Ukpo Improvement Union; Nze'nOzo, Ojiana; Friends of Ukpo, Umu Ada, Umu Okpu; Ladies and Gentlemen.

Introduction

My decision to come home from a U S base to answer the call on me to serve as President General in Ukpo from December 29, 2005 is rooted on two compelling factors. One factor is the death of two leaders, Edwin Nweke and Patrick Okoye around whom political, economic and social lives of the people of Akaezi revolved. The sudden and unexpected deaths in quick succession of the two leaders left the Akaezi people bereft and in states of confusion and hopelessness expressed in gloomy and tearful faces worn over an extended period of time. By then I had learnt that genuine tears is the true holy water, wiping genuine tears from the eyes of the deprived amounts to swimming in holy water.

Another factor is the compelling need to give back to Ukpo for the fortune of my life for which Ukpo prepared me. I was born a member of the Uzodinma Age Grade; in that generation a child growing up was a collective responsibility. Any adult could call to order a child who acted in a socially unaccepted manner. A hungry child could eat just by waiting for food to be ready in any nearby kitchen.

My formative primary education was dual: literacy and Christian religious moral. At St Simon's Catholic Church and School people such as Augustine Esedo, John Mezue, Anthony Onyeka and Godfrey Paul Mary Okoye influenced me. At St Mary's Anglican Church and School

---

[64] An address by the President General, Ukpo Improvement Union to IgweDr R. C. Eze, Okofia VI, Eze Ukpo on the occasion of the Igwe's 17th Ofala festival on December 20, 2008 at the Dunukofia Palace, Ukpo, Dunukofia.

the influences of Emmanuel Onuegbu, John Achebe and Catechist Chife were profound. Michael Eze, Sergeant Adibe, Nathaniel Okeke, Bertram Okpokwasili I, Levi Nwangwu, Ernest Igweilo, Gideon Otubelu, Walter Eze, Silvanus Nwako, Eric Okoye, Okwuchukwu Ezeaku and Fred Ezedinma were powerful role models in shaping my life.

Action Plan

In our UIU (Ukpo Improvement Union) we set out to accomplish what we considered priority needs in Ukpo which we unveiled on December 29, 2005. These were in the popular areas of education, health, and water supply, i.e. the so called amenities, which are government responsibilities. However, more important on our priority list were security of lives and property, especially security of the towns territory. Visible measures to show appreciation for the past heroes of the town were also on our priority list.

Overwhelmed by too much responsibilities, the UIU advertently suspended action on water supply and on erection of commemorative monuments. But through the aggressive efforts of the UIU health committee under the leadership of Elias Okafor, the UIU expanded the town's health facilities significantly from one health post to six and from one health center to two. In the education sector, the UIU education committee under the chairmanship of Godson Ofora worked closely with Chinyere Okunna, Vincent Ilora and the Lagos Youth League of the UIU to rehabilitate several school buildings, build computer and science laboratories and provide security in our various schools.

For close to 30 years, Ukpo has been fighting court battles in defense of the territorial integrity of the town in two fronts. At the beginning of the present UIU on December 29, 2005 the battles were dormant. Enjoying temporary legal advantages, opponents occupied the disputed areas. The UIU pursued these court cases with renewed vigor throughout the three year period.

While the UIU was pursuing the above defined action plan it became obvious that there were more basic needs that called for attention. For example, Ukpo culture was rapidly fading because as I said last year in this forum, certain Christian bigots vilified the Ukpo culture as satanic. When such zealots within the UIU opposed effort on the matter of cultural revival, some patriots led by Eric Omejilichi organized the FPC (Forum for the Promotion of Culture). In the past three years the forum has been effective in reviving the cultural values of the town to the extent that last month, Ukpo provided three of the 23 cultural troupes that represented Anambra State in the 2008 National Carnival in Abuja, the rest of 177town unions in the state provided the remaining 20 troupes.

Following the denigration of Ukpo culture as satanic, sacred forests and other public spaces became vulnerable to abuse by encroachment and poaching. This situation exposed the town dangerously to water and wind erosions. Additionally, deadly health hazards were accepted through what psychologists might describe as "normalizing the abnormal". The streets were normal dumps for garbage and sewage and people competed in all night operation of loud speakers at funerals, marriages, crusades and other celebrations. The consequent sudden and avoidable sicknesses and deaths were ignorantly attributed to human enemies next door or to retributive justice from offended gods.

The UIU enacted and strictly enforced six bylaws which effectively discouraged the flagrant exploitation of communal interests by private interests. Encroachment and poaching in public forests and spaces, dumping garbage and sewage in the streets, and advertising with loud speakers over the night skyline have no cost to the individuals. However costs to the community in terms of sickness, deaths, etc. due to noise and environmental pollutions are staggering.

Appreciation

Several Ukpo people including Paul Okeke, Chris Ayolugbe, Eric Udemba, Ernest Okeke, Emma Ekee, Bertram Okpokwasili II and about eighty others made significant financial contributions towards the UIU work. Money is not equal, i.e. one Naira is not equal to one Naira; it depends on among others how the money came. I do not forget a phone call one evening from Gideon Okpokwasili requesting UIU account number into which he deposited 100,000 Naira unsolicited.

The UIU cannot thank the Eze family too much for financial and psychological support in the past three years when Arthur Eze alone paid a disproportionately large share of the UIU expenses. But even then, the money Arthur gave directly to the UIU though large does not compare with his overall spending for the people of Ukpo which has been monumental. Last year in this forum, I stated that he spent over 100 million Naira in Ukpo on road construction, scholarships, renovation of Oye Market square. etc. in 2007 alone.

This year 2008 Arthur spent millions on renovation of churches, especially St Mary's Church which according to church goers now compares with standard church buildings in places such as New York. Most recently, he spent six million Naira to provide electricity and water supplies for the Nnamdi Azikiwe University Teaching Hospital and for the public. Recently, he spent 2.5 million Naira to resuscitate the Anambra State government abandoned public water system. Arthur's spending for Ukpo people is so much that it is difficult to keep record of.

Several Ukpo people supported the UIU effort in many other ways. Some put in full time effort running errands and others put their lives on line for Ukpo causes. Only yesterday by launching his scholarship foundation, Sebastian Adibe joined a young club which is emerging in Ukpo, namely scholarship foundations. Existing members of this compassionate club are Arthur Eze and Chinyere Okunna. I am confident that these two pioneers are glad to welcome Dr Sebastian Adibe to their club membership.

I call to mind the presence in Ukpo of a special school for orphans of HIV victims. The school is funded by USAID (United States Agency for International Development) through Winrock International and run by the Rural Women Foundation. This project which provides the children with not only literacy but also food supplements is often threatened by withdrawal of the USAID funding. Down on my knees I plead with people of good heart and means to contribute financially to support this Project of Compassion because it is a worthy cause.

Looking Ahead

On December 29 this year, i.e. nine days from today, there will be a new UIU in Ukpo. Without doubt, certain things will be done differently. But since the members of the new UIU were carefully selected following the constitutional guideline there is no doubt that in the next three years Ukpo is in good hands. I am confident that Ukpo people including members of the outgoing UIU will support the incoming one as much as they supported the outgoing one.

Conclusion

Igwe, I conclude by thanking you and your cabinet, Ukpo people in general and Akaezi people in particular for the opportunity to give back to the town and its people for my very life.

Documents Consulted

1. Ukpo Improvement Union Minutes of Meetings from 29th December 2006 to 29th December 2008.
2. Motion Against UIU Taking a Leading Role in Opoto Festival 2008 addressed to PG and all members of the UIU Executive. January 23, 2008 by Nwachala Ifeaka E.
3. Re-Your Letter to Parish Priest, St Simon's Parish, Ukpo with Regards to "the 2007 Opotor Festival in Ukpo addressed to the President General/Secretary General, Ukpo Improvement Union, Ukpo by Ilokolobia, Ignatious E.
4. Re-2007 Opotor Festival in Ukpo addressed to the President General, Ukpo Improvement Union, Ukpo. On February 1, 2007 by Rev Canon G. N. Oji.
5. The 2007 Opotor Festival in Ukpo addressed to the Parish Priest, St Simons Catholic Church, Ukpo on January 30, 2007 by Felix Nweke and Emma Nwankwo.
6. Secure Your Fatherland and be Counted Addressed to Prof Felix Nweke on August 25, 2005 by R. C. Eze and G. E. Okeke.
7. Re: SOS!!! addressed to Felix Nweke on October 9, 2007 by Kanayo Ejcm.
8. Re: [Ukpo Forum] Property Development in Ukpo addressed to My Dear Towns folks on October 9, 2007 by Kanayo Ejem.
9. Re: Re: Property Development in Ukpo addressed to Anayo on October 17, 2007 by Prof.
10. Professor Nweke is Spreading Malicious Rumors About Me addressed to the Igwe in Council, Dunukofia Palace, Ukpo on October 24, 2008 by Kanayo Ejem.
11. Professor Nweke is Spreading Malicious Rumors About Me: A Response by Professor Nweke. November 5, 2008.
12. Crusade! Crusade!! Crusade!!! by Innocent Agunwa and Josephat Okafor.
13. Letter of Petition addressed to President General, UIU on December 30, 2006 by I. Agunwa, Jude I. Dike and Chuka Oguno.
14. --------------- addressed to the Priest/Pastor in Charge on February 4, 2007 by Felix Nweke (for) and Emma Nwankwo.
15. Defiance of Town Union Constitution at St Simon's Catholic Church, Ukpo Dunukofia, January 11, 2008 by Felix Nweke.

16. ----------------addressed to Ignatious Ilokolobia on February 27, 2006 by William Onyeyili.
17. Re: Letter of Petition addressed to Catholic Charismatic Renewal, St Simon Catholic Church, Ukpo on January 1, 2007 by Ifeaka Nwachala.
18. Disruption of Catholic Crusade in Ukpo addressed to Felix Nneke on January 16, 2008 by IkediUgokwe.
19. In the High Court of Anambra State of Nigeria, In the High Court of Otuocha Judicial Division Holden at Otuocha Before His Lordship Hon. Justice V. N. Umeh on Wednesday the 16th of November 2011. Suit No. A/174/1995. Judgment Order by Obadiegwu, D. M.
20. In the Court of Appeal, Enugu Judicial Division Holden at Enugu (CA/E/30/2009) Suit No. A/11/75 and A/11/77 Consolidated. Certificate as to Non-Compliance with Conditions upon a would be Appellant 05-03-09 by Registrar and A. O. Otaluka.
21. In the Court of Appeal, Enugu Judicial Division Holden at Enugu Suit No. AA/53/75 and Consolidated AA/11/77 Appeal No. CA/E/195M/2005. Motion on Notice for the Following Order: by V. A. O. Omage.
22. In the Court of Appeal, Enugu Judicial Division Holden at Enugu on Tuesday the 13th of January 2009 before their Lordships .... CA/E/195M/2005 by A. O. Otaluka.
23. In the Supreme Court of Nigeria Holden at Abuja, Suit Nos. AA/53/75 and AA/11/77 (Consolidated), Appeal No. CA/E/161M/2004 SC/104/2005. Plaintiffs/Respondents' on Motion Dated 3/6/05 and Filed on 7/6/05. Dated this 23rd day of May 2006. By Wole Olanipeku (for).
24. In the High Court of Anambra State of Nigeria, In the High Court of Awka Judicial Division Holden at Awka before His Lordship Justice J. C. Igu on Monday 2nd day of June 2008. Suit No. A/236/2004. Judgement. By. Osieme.
25. In the High Court of Anambra State of Nigeria, In the High Court of Awka Judicial Division Holden at Awka before His Lordship Justice F. C. Nwizu on Tuesday the 10th day of May 2005 A/236/2005. F. C. Nwizu.
26. In the High Court of Anambra State of Nigeria, In the High Court of Awka Judicial Division Holden at Awka. Statement of Claim. Dated this 29th day of April 2005. C. a. Asadu.

27. Has Otimgbodomgbo Road Become a Failed Contract and an Abandoned Project? To Governor Peter Obi, 28th August 2006. Felix Nweke and Ifeaka Nwachala.

28. Data Capture on the Present State of Dilapidation of the Road Linking KM0+000 Beginning from Oye-Agu Abagana up to K M4+960 at Ukpo Junction on the Enugu-Onitsha Expressway. 12th June 2006.

29. Delimitation of Federal Constituencies: Situating Dunukofia Local Government Area to the Chairman Independent National Electoral Commission, Abuja, 18th July 2008. R. C. Eze.

30. UIU Resolutions: Conservation of Public Spaces. To the Secretary Igwe-in-Council. 24/05/07. Nwachala Ifeaka.

31. Ukpo Bylaws 2007, Ukpo Dunukofia. To Chairman Dunukofia Local Government. August 6, 2008. R. C. Eze and Felix Nweke.

32. Position of President General, Ukpo Improvement Union. To Raphael Akude. June 26, 2008. Felix Nweke.

33. Position of President General, Ukpo Improvement Union. To Felix Nweke. 28th June 2008. Raphael Akude.

34. End of Year (2003) Activities in Ukpo: A Trial. To Vicar St Mary's Church, Ukpo; the Rev Father, St Simon's Churcch, Ukpo; President General, UIU Ukpo; the Chairmen Oranto, Isiekwulu, Akpuamd Akaezi Village Meetings; and R. C. Eze. 11-12-03, Max. Nwobo.

35. --------------- To Ukpo People. 23rd December 2006. R. C. Eze and Felix Nweke.

36. Regulated End of Year Activities: A Reminder. Max. Nwobor.

37. Report. Constitution Review Committee on the Rotation of Offices of Ukpo Improvement Union (UIU).

38. UIU-2008: Proposed Projects ad Estimated Cost. 2nd January 2008. Ukpo Improvement Union (UIU).

39. Ukpo individual contributions, 2006 to 2008 and January to July 8, 2009.

40. Request for Change of School Name. To President General, Ukpo Improvement Union, Ukpo. 17th Oct. 2006. Enemuo, I. I. and Okeke, P. C. Anambra State School System.

41. Change of School Name. To the Secretary Ukpo Improvement Union, Ukpo. 15th Feb. 2007. C. C. Eze.

42. Consideration for the 2007/2008 Award of the AdmoraOkunna Foundation Scholarships. To Stella C. Okunna. 14th January 2008.

43. Hand Over Note from the Chairman UIU Health Committee: Hon.Elias Okafor. To the President General. 15th December 2008. Hon Elias A. Okafor.

44. An Address by the President General of Ukpo Improvement Union on the Occasion the thirteenth Ofala Festival of H. R, H. (Dr) R. C. Eze Okofia VI, Eze Ukpo-Dunukofia this Day, 23/12/04. Gibson Okeke.

45. Goodwill Message by H. R. H. Igwe Dr. R. C. Eze, Okofia VI, Eze Ukpo Dunukofia, at the 13th Ofala on Wednesday, 23rd December, 2004, Dunukofia Palace, Ukpo. R. C. Eze.

46. Mutual Respect among Leadership Institutions at Ukpo. December 16, 2006. Felix Nweke.

47. Dividends of Progressive Leadership at Ukpo. Felix Nweke.

48. Self-Determined Cultural Imperialism: A Drag on Progress Towards Social Justice in Ukpo-Dunukofia. December 22, 2007. Felix Nweke.

49. A Call from Home to Serve December 20, 2008. Felix Nweke.

50. Time for Intervention is Now. The Concerned Citizens of Ukpo.

51. Thank You. 24th December 2011. Ofodile Okafor.

52. The Holy Bible, New International Version. 1973, 1978, 1984 by International Bible Society. Exodus 20 page 56.

53. Ada ObodoOfor Returns Where She Came, A Profile and Tributes to Joy Mgbafocha Onyeyili-Nweke. Nancy Achebe, Editor. 2004. (No publisher).

54. Ukpo Improvement Union (UIU) Audit Report Part 2 Content-Audited Report, Observations and Recommendation (March 2013 to May 2014)

55. Ezebube, Chukwurah. 1992. The making of the Owelle of Ichida: The success story of Owelle G. P. O. Chikelu. Matterson Ltd, Lagos. xiv+259.

56. Estes, Clarissa Pinkola. 1995. Women who run with the wolves: Myths and stories of the wild woman archetype. Ballantine Books. New York.

57. Prof Felix Nweke. Appointment of President General of Ukpo Improvement Union (UIU). To Igwe in-Council, Care of the Cabinet Secretary, Ukpo, Dunukofia. Copy: Secretary General, Ukpo Improvement Union (UIU). October 22, 2013.

58. Ukpo individual contributions, 2006 to 2008 and Jan to July 8, 2009.

59. History of Ukpo Improvement Union by Eric Omejilichi, unpublished.

Index

www.ingramcontent.com/pod-product-compliance
Lightning Source LLC
Chambersburg PA
CBHW061749270326
41928CB00011B/2434